Ensuring Success for All Students:  Programs that Work

# Ensuring Success for All Students: Programs that Work

*by John W. Dougherty*

National Middle School Association
Columbus, Ohio

**National Middle School Association**
**2600 Corporate Exchange Drive, Suite 370**
**Columbus, Ohio 43231**
**NMSA** Telephone (800) 528-NMSA

Sue Swaim, Executive Director
Jeff Ward, Director of Business Services
John Lounsbury, Editor
Mary Mitchell, Copy Editor/Designer
Marcia Meade, Publications Sales

ISBN: 1-56090-115-2    NMSA Stock Number: 1243

**Library of Congress Cataloging-in-Publication Data**
Dougherty, John W.
    Ensuring success for all students: programs that work/ by John W. Dougherty.
        p.    cm.
    Includes bibliographical references (p. ).
    ISBN 1-56090-115-2
    1. Underachievers--Education--United States--Case studies.
 2. Socially handicapped children--Education--United States--Case studies. 3. Student adjustment--United States--Case studies.
 4. Educational counseling--United States--Case studies. 5. Academic achievement--United States--Case studies.  I. Title.
    LC4691.D68   1997
    371.93'08694--dc21                                    97-8717
                                                              CIP

To my wife, Francie, for always being patient and understanding; our daughter, Melissa, for giving me insight into middle school students; and our son, James, for perfecting my perceptions.

# Contents

# Preface

Ensuring Success For All Students: Programs That Work was created to assist middle school educators in establishing programs that support the middle school philosophy. It was also designed to encourage the examination of programs and practices that may be detrimental to the students in the schools. While the programs were designed for middle schools, many may find application in the elementary and secondary schools.

This publication is largely a description of the efforts of teachers at Hazelwood Junior High School in Florissant, Missouri, where the author previously served as principal. These programs and practices can be replicated in any school or district. Hazelwood Junior High School teachers recognized the validity of the middle school philosophy and conscientiously developed programs that would enable all students to be more successful.

I would like to thank two people for their help in producing this monograph:

— My colleague, Jeanne Donovan, for editing expertise and for making many valuable suggestions.

— My new friend, John H. Lounsbury, for his help in editing and managing the production of this book.

— John W. Dougherty

*We can whenever and wherever we choose successfully teach all children whose education is of interest to us. We already know more than we need to do that. Whether we do it or not must finally depend upon how we feel about the fact that so far we haven't.* — Ronald Edmunds

# Foreword

These words of the late Ronald Edmunds cut to the heart. The truth, we know, hurts. Rationalizations for continuing business as usual are readily available. Some hide in unquestioned assumptions about the nature of intelligence and the well-entrenched ways of conducting education. Others reside in certification policies, budget limitations, the expectation of parents, and even the way we build and furnish schoolrooms. Apathy and the security of doing what we are accustomed to doing also play a part.

Yet the fact that our public schools are failing significant numbers of young adolescents is all too obvious to those who stop to examine current practices honestly and thoroughly. So too is the hard-to-accept truth that Dr. Edmunds stated in the above quote. The problem is more in our will – or lack of it – than in our lack of knowledge.

Fortunately there are schools and faculties that have taken the challenge and instituted programs that help to secure success for all students. One such school is the Hazelwood Junior High School where the author, John Dougherty, was principal. In this book he speaks directly about three underlying issues and then describes several programs that were directed at solving recognized school shortcomings and would result in more students achieving success.

The precept "all kids can learn" is easily verbalized and endorsed. It is currently a popular idea, but it is one that continues to be countered by long-standing school practices that reflect a different assumption about the intellectual capacities of young people. It is particularly important at this time in our history that middle level schools continue their pioneering work in creating programs and arrangements that will put into practice this belief in the universality of learning potential. Too long schools have been more successful in carrying out a sorting and selecting function than they have in guaranteeing success for all students.

While the programs described in this volume may not be unique, they are real – and they achieved their goal of bringing school success to an increasing percentage of the students at that school. Use these descriptions to stimulate your thinking and planning on the local level. Examine honestly the implicit lessons your school teaches by its programs and policies. And where those lessons make it evident that success is all but denied some students, be willing to initiate efforts that will broaden the base. The examples in this volume deserve to be examined, adapted, and/or used as springboards for creating programs that will bring academic success to all your students.

—John H. Lounsbury

# Introduction

*Sometimes the school needs to change so
the students may change.* — Bobbitt

Every day thousands of young people enter the doors of our schools. Many are very successful while some are not. Some are successful over the long haul but not for a day or a week. Some are successful for a period but are not for their school career. Success and/or failure in school is much like a physical or mental illness. Some of us are sick for a while, and others are chronically ill all of the time. This analogy leads to the sobering conclusion that every student runs the risk of experiencing at least a temporary or perhaps a permanent disconnection from productive learning in school (Sinclair & Ghory, 1987).

The school must provide programs for the chronically unsuccessful student, and it must also have programs that can support the occasionally at-risk young person. These experiences must be available to every student, because all are capable of being successes and/or failures.

Educators, as advocates of youth, can and should take the lead in efforts to ensure that every young person has the opportunity to achieve a piece of the American dream.

This book was written to offer suggestions to those educators who desire that all students succeed in school all of the time. It offers insights into programs that have enjoyed success in some schools and could provide a structure for developing beneficial programs for other schools.

Our schools must be institutions of hope for all children. Kuykendall (1992) says, "An effective teacher can give a child hope. With hope, there is reason to look to tomorrow. Without hope, life is meaningless. Without hope, there is greater propensity for negative behavior" (p. xv). Education is a profession of hope, and perhaps this book can increase the reader's hope of meeting the needs of all students.

*Ensuring Success for All Students: Programs That Work* provides the reader descriptions of programs that could be established in any school to help all young people be successful. It also gives an overview of some issues that are essential in understanding, relating to, and teaching young adolescents. Those characteristics existing in schools that contribute to making children unsuccessful and ways to eliminate them or negate their impact are reviewed.

The first three chapters in this book raise philosophical questions about issues that were the driving force behind the programs outlined in the last seven chapters. Programs in schools often address symptoms and not the philosophical or psychological components of schools or society that may be producing the maladies. As principal, I saw it as part of my leadership role that all programs should address the philosophical as well as the pragmatic.

The last seven chapters tell the reader about approaches or programs that have been used to help meet the needs of kids, all kids. These are not research-based programs based on tons of objective data supporting their success, and I don't know if raising a grade from a twenty percent to a fifty-five percent, both "F" grades, is being successful or not. If the reader can identify a program as a possibility for meeting the needs of students in his/her school, then this effort is worthwhile, and the reader can decide upon the success or failure of the program in each individual setting.

Many of our children are unsuccessful because of the very efforts that schools make to help them. The courses that are remedial in nature are designed to help the "slow" learner, the potential dropout, etc. but in reality these courses often become a contributing factor to the failure of the child. This concern is addressed in Chapter 1.

Too many of our unsuccessful children are children of color. They carry a double burden. Not only are they susceptible to all of the other factors that contribute to being unsuccessful, but they also have the burdens of prejudice and discrimination. Institutional racism, as well as prejudice from classmates, gives the minority child many more opportunities to be less than what he/she could be in school. Chapter 2 is written to describe how these children may be assisted.

The third chapter is about the alienation of students, the socialization of young people, and ways schools can bring the two together to help all children be more successful.

In the fourth chapter, a look will be taken at the orientation program that is a child's initial introduction to a new school. Throughout this chapter, as in the others, there will be a focus on the child and the parents. None of us lives in isolation, and the school must impact the home and the out-of-school lives of students. The out-of-school time is three times longer than the time in school.

A summer transition program is discussed in Chapter 5. This is a program designed for students coming into the junior high or middle school. This program with modifications could also be used for ninth graders entering high school.

Much research has been done that relates the child's achievement to the extent of the parent's involvement in the school and its programs. Pigford (1992) says:

> I am convinced that the major difference between at-risk children and those not at-risk is their levels of dependency on the school experience. At-risk children, who are typically from lower social-class backgrounds, have limited resources on which they can rely and must therefore depend on the school to provide for and promote their academic, social, and psychological development. Children, not at-risk, typically those from middle- and upper-class backgrounds, have support structures within their families and home environments. The challenge for schools is first to identify children lacking support structures outside the school and then to provide the necessary support. — p. 155

How can parents be involved in a school's effort with the students? Chapter 6 will discuss two programs that are working to answer that question positively.

Advisory programs are examined in Chapter 7 and are viewed from the point of how they can prevent students from being just a number. Student advisory programs may be faddish for some and viewed with skepticism by others, but they are a way of reducing the sense of rejection that so many children feel, particularly in large schools.

Chapter 8 is devoted to an after school program that offers strong tutorial support for academics but also attempts to increase a child's self-esteem as well as help his/her study and organizational skills.

Chapter 9 deals with I-CANN, a program that provides counseling, development of self-esteem, and a hands-on curriculum for the potential failure. It is discussed as an alternative program that can be adapted to any school at any grade level.

You do not have to read this book from beginning to end. Find the chapter that addresses a need in your school and read it. Every program discussed is a single entity. However, the author firmly believes that everything is connected to everything else, and programs for kids in schools must be connected to all that the school does. So look for that spider web of connectedness both in the book and in the programs in your school.

These programs are not offered as panaceas for solving all the problems of young people. If they suggest approaches that the reader can adapt, then my purpose has been fulfilled. Gastright (1989) warns, "It has been tempting for some districts to fall back on stereotypical views of students. Educators who attempted to educate students on the basis of such stereotypes may have failed because they neglected local characteristics" (p. 1-4). Please modify anything in this book to fit your situation. If you want to talk to me about anything I have written, my address is:

John W. Dougherty, Associate Professor, Lindenwood College, 209 S. Kingshighway, St. Charles, MO 63301. Home: (314) 940 - 0770; Office: (314) 949-4937. ◾

# 1.
# Eliminating
# School Factors
# That Create
# Problems for Children

*Imagine how it would seem if our educational system evaluated students around the sixth grade and if you did not have clear potential for playing tennis at a Wimbledon championship level, the school and the parents would say you are not now and never will be a tennis player, and that would be the end of tennis for you.*
— Robert Fulghum

The educational concepts guiding the development of the modern middle school have forced us to reexamine what we have been doing. We are making changes needed to prepare students for the 21st century, altering approaches, planning new programs, and becoming concerned with aspects of development that previously have not been the school's concern.

One characteristic of schools that few have really questioned until recently, has been that of tracking and the use of remediation with the lower ability groups. Remedial classes and the philosophy that spawned them are now being examined in terms of whether they help students or are actually, in fact, detrimental to them.

Educators have used labels to describe, characterize, classify, and segregate segments of the student population. Labeling has led to tracking and tracking has led to remediation. Unfortunately, labels often become oversimplified descriptions and are used to stereotype behaviors for all the individuals in particular groups (Brodbelt, 1991). Stevenson (1992) says that grouping students according to "ability measures" is no more justified than grouping them by shoe sizes. Tracking creates students who feel differently and who, hence, act differently.

Henry Levin (1990), a professor of education and economics at Stanford University, believes that traditional remedial classes that focus on students' weaknesses are self-defeating. The slower the classes go, the more the students get behind. Thus, once a child is placed in a remedial classes, he/she can never "catch up."

Nearly a quarter of America's children are in an educational path leading nowhere, claims Patricia Gandara (1989). She adds that the practice of tracking would be acceptable if the assumption on which it is based, that homogeneous grouping, simplified teaching, and encouraged superior learning were valid.

Proponents of remedial programs seem to have lost sight of the original goal of remediation, i.e., improved classroom learning. The notion that remedial students need different approaches has little to support it beyond tradition. Remedial programs that are not integrated with the core curriculum become isolated from the central efforts of the schools. If the remedial courses are not consistent with the main thrust of the school, then neither are the students enrolled in those classes. They become the alienated ones. Tracking perpetuates their isolation, places them further at risk, and increases the likelihood of their dropping out. Thus tracking has the potential for sabotaging healthy, optimistic identity formation among young adolescents whose capacities and abilities are in flux.

If remedial classes are viewed as opportunities to teach the regular curriculum to smaller groups of students and provide more individualized student instruction and teacher assistance, they might have merit. But a simple reduction in class size does not necessarily guarantee quality teaching or higher levels of achievement. Too often teachers use the same general approach in instructing regardless of class size or the achievement levels of the students.

Despite smaller class size, students in compensatory and remedial programs are seldom taught as a group in which the teacher explains material to a group of students followed by interaction with the teacher and one another asking questions and making comments (Rowan, Guthrie, Lee, & Guthrie, 1986). Remedial class teachers spend little instructional time actively or interactively teaching. Instead, the students spend large amounts of time working by themselves at their seats on written assignments. During this time, teachers circulate among the students, monitor their work, and provide tutoring as necessary (OERI, 1987; Anderson, Cook, Pellicer, & Spradling, 1989). Little student socialization or cooperation takes place.

Students in remedial and compensatory classes may have high success rates based on scores on written class work. Unfortunately, however, the cognitive demands placed on these students by the questions and worksheets are often far lower than those typically asked in other classes or on state or national tests. These data suggest that teachers teach to the students' present levels of academic functioning rather than to the levels they will need to achieve to be successful in the future (Rowan, et al., 1986; Anderson, et al., 1989). As a consequence, many compensatory and remedial students appear to be successful in the short term but remain largely unsuccessful over the long haul. The students soon become disenchanted because the school cannot provide them with the skills needed to succeed outside of the remedial classroom. Finally, compensatory and remedial programs rarely teach the development of higher order skills. Rather, their emphasis is on the acquisition of basic facts and skills (Pogrow, 1990). According to Goodlad (1984), research shows that the actual range in performance in any group is consistently greater than the organizational arrangement assumes and portrays. If all of the above is true and there is little evidence that remediation and tracking of students into lower levels for remediation does any academic good, then students in those programs become frustrated for naught. Frustration with school and a sense of being incompatible with the school and its programs alienates many students. The school, then, becomes a major contributor to creating dropouts.

O'Neil (1991) believes that a commonly cited barrier to greater student motivation is an atmosphere of low expectations and a watered down curriculum that results from schools' efforts to track students. Students as early as first grade, where ability based reading groups appear, are aware of whether teachers consider them to be of high or low ability. This stratification is wrong. The First Curriculum Congress established 15 themes for guiding future curriculum, teaching, and learning. One of these calls for heterogeneous grouping of students as all the recent curriculum documents unequivocally call for ending tracking and greatly reducing ability grouping (Steffens, 1990).

Tracking, however, is still a pervasive practice in public education. Slavin (1989) found in a review of the literature highly positive results for mixed-ability grouping for remedial and average students. Remedial programs do not achieve the results anticipated nor hoped for and they increase the at-risk factors for students. Noland and Taylor (1986) believe not only does the practice of ability grouping not increase student achievement, it also has adverse effects on students' self-concept. Once judged as inferior individuals start acting inferior – the self-fulfilling prophecy takes over. Once a pupil is tracked, he or she often carries that label throughout the schooling experience. In New York City only one out of thirty special education children were ever returned to a regular school program (Haskins, Walden, & Ramsey, 1983).

Students in the lower tracks, then, travel in a pack, seeing each other's failures, reinforcing each other's less desirable traits, imitating each other's poor work habits, and copying each other's undisciplined behaviors. No wonder that such students are unsuccessful and eventually drop out. No wonder they develop a passive orientation to learning, the very mental set that educators try to avoid with students. If educators are to tackle the problem of learned helplessness they must address the crucial task of improving student self-perceptions, for unless students can see themselves as capable of tackling a task, their chances for success are seriously diminished.

Tracking denies lower-placed students the basic right to equality of schooling. When Goodlad (1984) looked closely at tracked groupings, he found that the crucial difference between high and low groups constituted a marked inequality in access to knowledge; that ability tracking creates an "instructionally disadvantaged" subclass of students in our schools as we set for them a different course content, encourage different teacher behaviors and attitudes, and relate and respond differently as teachers.

Oakes (1985) reached these conclusions on the practice of tracking:

- There is little evidence to support the standard rationale offered in defense of tracking – that is, the needs of students are better met when they learn in groups with similar capacities or prior levels of achievement.
- There are "remarkable and disturbing differences" between classes in different tracks in terms of student access to knowledge, classroom instructional opportunities, and classroom learning environment.
- Students who are not in top tracks suffer "clear and consistent" disadvantages from tracking.
- The net effect of tracking is to exaggerate initial differences among students in terms of academic achievement and future aspirations.
- Placement in lower tracks begins a cycle of restricted opportunities and diminished outcomes that tends to reduce self-esteem, lower aspirations, and foster negative attitudes toward school.
- Tracking tends to prevent rather than promote the achievement of educational goals. — pp. 6-10

Most significantly, Goodlad (1984) found that instruction of heterogeneous groupings – classes that include students achieving at all levels – did not sink to the lower levels associated with the lower tracked students. Rather, classes containing a heterogeneous mixture of students "were more like high than low track classes in regard to what students were studying, how teachers were teaching, and how teachers and students were interacting." When tracking is done away with, conventional wisdom would predict that because significantly more students are enrolled in both accelerated and regular levels, grades should tend to be lower and requests for downward level changes more frequent. The exact opposite occurs (DuFour & Schwartz, 1990).

Despite all the evidence, tracking remains common in schools across the country. Whatever terms it is couched in, the bottom line is usually the contention that schools are meeting each individual's academic needs by grouping homogeneously. Tracking persists, in part because it makes the status quo easier to maintain. However much teachers might talk about "providing for individual differences," tracking at best exists for the benefit of teachers and the listening/work mode. At worst, tracking allows educators to blame students when the school has failed to teach them well.

It doesn't have to be this way. To persuade adolescent students of their academic potential, they must believe they can succeed. It must be demonstrated that teachers believe every student has academic potential. Students need more able peer models; they need to be surrounded by other students whose ideas will spark and charge the environment, and they generally need more individualized attention. No matter what the teacher's expectations, if he/she has a class of twenty-five low achieving students, it will be hard to inspire the group or to provide the individual response needed. But if the instructor has a handful of low ability students in every class, those students can catch fire from the enthusiasm generated by the other students, and the teacher can give them the extra time they need as he/she circulates among the students.

Students tracked into the top groups now see their classmates as competitors; measuring themselves against fast-learning friends, they often worry that they're not smart enough to warrant inclusion and panic over grades. Tracking can, thus, create very anxious young people in the upper strata as well. Students placed in the bottom groups are smart enough to look around the first week of school and catch on – "I'm in the dumb group; I'll be here forever, and I know little is expected of me." They also catch on to who's in the top group when students from other sections describe their courses and homework – activities more challenging, interesting, and worthwhile. Students placed in lower homogeneous sections are the ones most in need of interesting, challenging, and worthwhile instruction. They most need the school to be enlightening and to make sense. They most of all need coaching, but they mostly get routine remedial work, low-level texts and low-level ideas, and teachers faced with a crazy situation – a whole class of students who need help but mostly get managed and disciplined.

## Conclusion

The decision to eliminate tracking and ability grouping as well as the remediation that usually accompany those practices must be made if the schools themselves are to stop creating unsuccessful students. Such a decision is supported by considerable research, informed opinion, and plain common sense. Remedial instruction has failed to bring the performance of low-achieving students up to the level of their classmates. Rather, remedial course work tends to slow students down, partly as a result of low expectations on the part of teachers. Eliminating remedial courses will raise expectations for these students and help ensure that they will graduate with the skills and knowledge they need for success.

Tracking that inevitably calls for remediation must also be ended. Contemporary society demands a high level of thinking and personal competence, goals that cannot be accomplished in tracked classes. To ensure success for all students, schools must phase out tracking. ▪s

*The justification for ensuring education for all of our citizens through public funds is in large measure an expression of belief in the importance of every person's life.*
            — Stevenson, 1992
*I hear the human race is falling on its face.*      — from *South Pacific*
*We Americans are children of the crucible.*
          — Theodore Roosevelt

# 2.
# The Colorization of Educational Programs

The largest single group of at-risk young people in school are children of color. Not only do all of the characteristics of the at-risk youth describe many minority students but they have the additional alienating factor called prejudice. Discrimination, institutional racism, and the attitude of society at-large place additional burdens on minority children. For these young people schools must not only alleviate the usual school contributors to their being unsuccessful, but they must integrate them into the total school life. School programs that do not integrate all children are, like tracking, unacceptable. Achieving an integrated education goes beyond mere desegregation. It implies an easy incorporation into the educational process of multicultural groups that is undergirded by a genuine respect for all.

The demographics of most parts of the United States are changing rapidly. By the year 2020, the population of the United States will be 30 percent Black and Hispanic (US Census Bureau, 1990). Several states already have "minority" populations that are in the majority. In many large metropolitan school systems, the majority of the students are children of color. The Census Bureau estimates that 42 percent of all public school children will come from these racial "minorities" in 2000.

Benning (1992) gives us the following information:
- Nationally, public schools enroll about 61 million students; private schools enroll just over 8 million.

- Nationally, in 1976 minorities made up 24 percent of the public school enrollment; by 1986, the percentage had grown to nearly 30 percent, and by 1991 was about 33 percent. Minority percentages are expected to grow more rapidly in the near future.
- Minorities tend to be concentrated in the cities, with their proportions there likely to increase.
- Birthrates are highest for people having the least education and lowest incomes, and vice versa.
- The birthrates of minority middle classes are indistinguishable from the birthrates of white middle-class people. For the most part, birthrates tend to be color blind. However, birthrates are sensitive to economic status. — p. 3

Society, and particularly the schools, must address the issue of children potentially being unsuccessful because they are not white. Failure to do so will result in an ever increasing number of people unable to contribute adequately to society and likely headed to becoming school dropouts.

Schools are unknowingly, or unwittingly, structured to fail certain kinds of students. When schools are organized around white, middle class values, many students of different ethnic or economic backgrounds do not feel welcome. Their dress, appearance, and even the way they have been taught to communicate and reason is mysteriously and subtly "wrong" when they get to school. The gap between the kinds of behaviors tolerated at home and the behavior acceptable at school widens, as does the gap between parents and teachers. Students who feel unwelcome, uncomfortable, and/or incompetent often react by leaving the situation, either physically (initiating the cycle of truancy, suspension, dropping out) or psychologically. Students drop out, or are pushed out, by a system that just doesn't mean anything to them. The lack of connections between the curriculum and what the students view as "real life" is so great as to be unbridgeable. Schools must breach the gap between education and life outside of school.

The American public school dropout rate is said to be 25 percent, and as high as 40 percent in urban areas (Strother, 1986). Blacks are dropping out at the rate of one out of four, Hispanics are leaving at the rate of one out of three, and Whites at the rate of one out of seven (Calabrese, 1988).

African American, Latino, Hispanic, American Indian, and poor children, in general, continue to achieve below grade level, drop out in much greater numbers, and go to college in much lower proportion than their middle-class and European-American peers (Nieto, 1992). Programs must be initiated that will reverse this trend.

What does the school do or not do that causes the students of color to be unsuccessful because of their skin pigmentation? Educational systems probably do not do anything intentionally to promote students' lack of success, but are they presently doing anything to help the situation? Multicultural programs are often seen as a means of alleviating discipline problems rather than a viable way of helping young people learn academics.

In the previous chapter remedial programs and tracking were identified as programs that label students. Brodbelt (1991) claims that power groups use labeling to stigmatize and paralyze the powerless groups; an example of this phenomenon is the labeling of blacks as mentally and morally inferior persons. The public school system often has reflected this attitude by tending to track African Americans and other minority students into classes that are below standard, leading them to drop out or be denied higher education and limited success in the job market. This not only alienates students, it is institutional racism.

The concept of "blaming the victim" comes into play when the person who is labeled eventually comes to feel that he deserves the label that justifies unequal treatment and its negative classification. Obviously, such a label is detrimental to self-esteem, resulting in loss of self-confidence and self-respect. Dropping out then becomes a viable solution, a last ditch means of retaining one's limited self-esteem and having some control.

If tracking is eliminated, children of color will less often be placed in untenable positions. They will then experience environments where many viewpoints are expressed, various lifestyles are evident, all sorts of abilities and disabilities are accepted, and an enjoyment and appreciation of differences flourishes.

The climate of the school, its collective attitude toward the minority youngster must be conducive to the education and self-esteem of that child. The structure of schools generally reflects the culture of middle class students not that of minority students. The structure of most schools does not cater to the needs of Black, Chicano, Asian, Native American, or other ethnic and cultural groups. Schools with high minority enrollments tend to be more custodial in nature and offer a curriculum designed to orient students toward blue-collar occupations. The message

14

to minority youngsters is that they must accept these values, conform, or drop out (Beck & Muria, 1980). Teachers contribute to this culture by focusing on strict punitive discipline, holding low student expectations, and embarrassing or humiliating them. Often these actions are supported or ignored by the administration. The attitudes of adults responsible for programs in schools must change if all students are to be successful.

Teachers create a nourishing environment characterized by intimacy and fruitfulness only to the extent their own ethos mirrors these qualities. Consequently, administrators must welcome staff members each day, reinforce them for the good things they do for children all day long, provide support for the new teachers, ensure that personnel evaluations are carried out in a helpful spirit, model effective problem-solving and conflict resolution behaviors, support teachers in their efforts to pursue professional growth, and involve them in program decision making (Rogus & Wildenhaus, 1991). Everyone must support and care for everyone else.

What can the school system do? Some teachers have to be helped to alter their attitudes toward minority children. Administrators have to focus on the system and its failures in regard to the minority student. There has to be a sense of fairness and justice apparent by offering an equitable education to all children. Schools cannot project the image that public education is designed primarily for middle and upper class students.

Creating a climate that is inviting to all students is important for everyone, but especially important for the potential dropout and the student of color. Rogus and Wildenhaus (1991) believe that it is therefore vital that teachers:

- Welcome students to class each day.
- Learn names quickly and address students by their first names as often as possible.
- Seek one-to-one contact with students between classes, during lunch periods, and after school.
- Acknowledge a student's return to class after an absence.
- Express frequently the view that "I am here to help you achieve and not to tell you that you didn't."
- Engage in no truces with students. (A truce is an unspoken agreement between teacher and student that "I won't bother you if you don't bother me.")                                        — pp. 3-4

### Student Leadership Forum

To combat racism, a good program to implement is one similar to the Student Leadership Forum developed by the Coloma, Michigan High School (Wheeler, 1991).

The purpose of the Student Leadership Forum is:

- Proactively dealing with students behaving in a manner counter-productive to positive racial interaction,
- Reactively dealing with other students when racial situations become acute and incidents take place (addressing problem situations),
- Serving as an informational source to teachers and administrators by providing feedback regarding the racial climate of the school in specific situations that could lead to racial problems,
- Serving as a sounding board to the administration for suggesting in-service needs of staff and students and reacting to proposed programs of the administration, and
- Involving parents in activities designed to eliminate stereotyping, improve race relations, and enhance the way desegregation is viewed.

To address these purposes, the Forum provides training in interpersonal and communication skills, group dynamics and effectiveness, problem solving, stereotyping, prejudice, and discrimination. The members are students representative of race, gender, grade level, and racial attitudes (positive and negative).

Members of the Forum established the following specific objectives:

- Encourage greater understanding and closer ties between people of different races, religions, gender, socio-economic backgrounds, and persuasions.
- Improve communications between the administration and students and between the faculty and students.
- Enhance the public's image of the school.
- Help solve inner-racial problems among students, between faculty and students, and between parents and students.

Wheeler says that the Forum has been able to deal effectively with acute racial situations and defuse potential problems. It also has been able to proactively foster enhanced African American-White interactions and relationships (p. 5).

## Conclusion

Teachers in our schools should use teaching strategies that address the distinctive traits of minority youngsters. Students perform at higher levels academically when instructional methods complement their learning characteristics and student-teacher relations reflect respect. Many teachers do not fully understand minority youngsters or what instructional techniques would be appropriate for them. Schools must be about the business of helping teachers develop the needed understandings and related instructional strategies.

Teaching about other cultures is difficult because the general population know little about other cultures and are influenced by stereotypical local and regional biases. Schools and principals can address this difficulty by offering staff development programs designed to target known intercultural interaction problem areas. By focusing on identified culturally based misunderstandings, and by jointly taking positive steps to rectify such misunderstandings, the negative aspects of blaming misunderstandings on one group or another is avoided.

Programs offered must not contribute to placing students at risk or alienating them by placing them in untenable positions. Often this does not require the development of new programs to ensure success for all young people, but simply abandoning practices that create barriers to their success. ◼S

*We can teach so that our students feel inferior, or so as to help them think better of themselves.* — Anonymous

*Every day, wittingly or unwittingly, we choose whether we want to be more or less humane, more or less human.*
— Edgar Dale

*Far and away the best prize that life offers is the chance to work hard at work worth doing.*
— Theodore Roosevelt

# 3.
# Alienation and Socialization of Students

Too many students are angry with, alienated from, and apathetic toward school. Mackey (1978) defines alienation as a feeling of separation and disconnectedness. Alienation is a form of disengagement marked by isolation, powerlessness, lack of meaning, and an unwillingness to accept societal norms (Calabrese, 1988). It is manifested in a student's poor attendance, cutting classes, tardiness, and a general negative attitude toward the school, the teachers, and the engaged students. To some degree this may be a result of an uncaring faculty, rules and regulations, and a school structure that emphasizes control rather than education.

Many students are alienated because schools, however unwittingly, reinforce the concept that public education is designed for middle and upper class students. School behaviors and attitudes that are often interpreted as apathy, boredom, or rebelliousness more likely are evidence that youngsters are not learning things that they care about and/or that instructional methods are not compatible with how they learn best (Stevenson, 1992). Analysis has demonstrated that adolescent alienation may be characterized by three independent and measurable dimensions: (1) personal incapacity, the feeling of incompetence in dealing with the social world; (2) guidelessness, the feeling that the rules of conduct have collapsed; and (3) cultural estrangement, the rejection of the predominant criteria for success (Mackey, 1977).

18

Culturally estranged students need to engage in learning activities that are intellectually honest, provide opportunities for analysis, and involve serious social issues. Education could reduce cultural estrangement by providing experiences in school governance and involving the students in curricular and instructional planning. Adequate guidance would result from students' having an awareness of social rules and customs, experiences in social settings, and the chance to test their understandings and skills in real situations.

In school, adolescents should learn about the nature of social rules and the mores that dominate the larger society. Teachers should try to communicate with young people in ways that penetrate their cultural barriers. Sensitive and perceptive educators must learn and recognize the language and nonverbal expressions of the youth culture although not adopt them as elements of their own culture. Failure to counter the alienation of some students leads to a deepening of that social disintegration and detachment.

According to Stevenson (1992), students should be able to hold three beliefs about schools.

1.	Young adolescents need to believe that their school is a place where they will receive fair treatment, where justice prevails, and where individuals have a right to speak their minds freely without fear of retribution – elements of our democratic American heritage that have already become part of their daily lives and expectations. They assume they will be governed by rules, and they expect the rules will be equitably derived, clearly articulated, and fairly enforced.

2.	High in their priorities is the need to believe that they will be safe at school, that order will prevail, and that they will not be victimized either physically or emotionally. They also should recognize that neither adults nor kids alone can accomplish the order they both value.

3.	Youngsters desperately need to believe that they will be successful at school and that by applying themselves through work they can achieve success. They come expecting to work but needing for that work to be understandable in terms of one's capability and reasonable in terms of volume. When work is thus doable, willingness to work follows. — p. 211

Brubaker (1991) offers three principles that he believes at-risk students must possess if they are to become even minimally successful:

**Principle 1:** At-risk students need to believe they are moving toward something better. Educators must use language that speaks to this need.

**Principle 2:** At-risk students need the security of structure and predictable adult behavior. These students also respect adults who are flexible under special circumstances.

**Principle 3:** At-risk students need caring adult leaders who create the conditions for students to accept responsibility for their own lives. — pp. 59-66

In their study of adolescent self-concepts and self-esteem, Beane and Lipka (1986) asked students who were successful at school to identify factors that they attributed to their success. One of the primary factors identified in this important study was "nice teachers." Although "nice" is in the eye of the beholder, most readers will easily translate it into their own understanding. Good programs will be ineffective if teacher attitudes are negating a program's influence. Negative teacher attitudes are noticed by students and may dent their desire to achieve causing students to adopt negative feelings about themselves. Usually, an individual's attitudes toward others closely parallels his/her attitude toward himself/herself. Teachers with limited experience with people of diverse cultures face a threatening unknown when they are placed with a diverse student population, and this anxiety is transmitted to children and parents. However, when alienated students realize that their teachers and principals do care about them as individuals with worth and dignity, their perceptions of themselves begin to change. With this change comes the beginning of feelings of self-worth, of "can do" instead of "can't do." The school is then seen as a helping place, not an institution that controls and suppresses.

When day after day students are subjected to classes that have no personal meaning for them and in which they cannot succeed, it is no wonder they become alienated and disengaged. A disproportionate number of such students get placed in vocational and other non-academic courses or are taught a watered-down version of the standard curriculum. Many students view restrictions, nitpicking rules, and the personal demands made on them by some staff members as unreasonable. They conclude school isn't for them. We do know, however, that a paramount reason young adolescents come to school is for the opportunity to socialize with other students. Schools need to exploit positively the peer socialization factor to combat alienation and as a vehicle for learning.

An eighth grader, who felt alienated from her school because its organization kept her separated from many of her friends, said cynically, "I think they're just trying to keep us away from each other so we'll stay confused." Schools have a function and teachers a task – to provide meaningful opportunities for active student participation in the spectrum of learning decisions in a nurturing, sustaining environment designed to foster personal autonomy.

"I didn't really enjoy using drugs in junior high school but they were the people who accepted me." This tragic example of the extremes one young girl went to in order to resolve a desperate need for affiliation and affirmation in a large, impersonal school illustrates the great value young adolescents place on belonging. Faculties can affect the school climate, students' relationships with each other, teachers' relationships with students and with each other, and the attention given to student concerns.

To achieve such a climate and the interpersonal relationships desired is a major task but a doable one. The school, however, must be ready to make operational changes that enhance student-teacher relationships and create an environment that nurtures collaboration and mutual trust among students and teachers.

There are a number of easily implemented interventions available to (a) promote more productive peer interactions; (cooperative learning, cross-age tutoring, and peer counseling), (b) develop positive teacher-student relationships (TESA staff development program and teacher advisory programs), and (c) provide more meaningful in-school experiences that increase students' sense of belonging (community volunteer projects, curricular treatment of meaningful topics, and an appeals process within the school).

Schools, for the most part, are highly structured places. The student whose home provides little structure finds the tight structure of the school intolerable. Schools in a democracy should reflect democratic values more than they typically have.

The bright, motivated student also has a problem with restrictions such as hall passes, bells, permission slips, homework assignments, and little free time. For many poorly motivated students with marginal skills and a family that doesn't promote education, the denial of the pleasures of life makes school seem like a prison. Not being allowed to chew gum, wear a hat, sport a comb, use street language, or make an impression on one's peers is not worth fighting to stay in school. Schools must help students respect their own heritage and others' as well, help them judge the appropriateness of various behaviors in different situations, and identify their strengths and interests and to build upon them. School expectations should be altered responsibly to accommodate cultural differences, provide alternative schools or programs, and teach staff and students to value each individual as a person of dignity and worth. Schools should also reflect the golden rule.

It is paramount that schools make it evident that all students are full-fledged members of the community, entitled to the care and respect of staff and peers. Students' moral worth and dignity must be affirmed through contact with teachers in athletics, music outings, and personal advising. Students must have some influence on the conception, execution, and evaluation of the learning activities themselves.

Unfortunately, children do not expect school to be connected to their lives or related to their personal desires and concerns. Life in school has always been teacher-centered, textbook-dominated, restrictive, impersonal, and rigid (Goodlad, 1984). School becomes an endurance contest for the students, and many students lack the perserverance to stay the course.

Reducing the alienation of students, particularly minority students, calls for reforms in the traditional structure of schooling and school policies and regulations. Schools must accommodate various cultures and views in order to reduce alienation. No one likes to sit on the sidelines. Slavin (1979) found that schools in which interracial cooperative contact was encouraged had good race relations, and those in which contact was discouraged, did not. Students who had been on an interracial sports team or had worked with a member of another race in class had more positive interracial attitudes than other students. Students must have the opportunity to cooperate and interact with each other. The teaching staff is responsible for providing these opportunities.

Teachers have to be assisted in analyzing the ways the system may fail some students. There are many teacher-controlled factors that can counter or prevent student alienation:
- knowing students' names
- showing interest in students
- knowing of students' outside of school interests
- treating students with respect

- being fair
- laughing at themselves and with students
- outstanding teacher
- enthusiastic and knowledgeable in content areas.

Those students who have been classified as at-risk, tend to be treated differently from high achievers. Alienation results. For example, sometimes these students are seated further away from the teacher, given less direct instruction, offered fewer opportunities to learn new material, and asked to do less work. Studies have shown that they are called on less often, and when questioned, only expected to respond with simple recall answers. Especially when grouped together in a class, at-risk students are criticized more frequently, given little praise, and engage primarily in skill and drill type activities that offer little excitement.

When students are treated this way, it is not surprising that their attitudes toward school are negative. Schools need to create a sense of fairness and justice by offering all students an equal education. Although the phrase "all students can learn" has become popular, it is not always reflected in practice. Many schools offer an equal "quantity" of education, but not equal "quality" of education. Students must have the same chance within individual classrooms as they do within the school generally.

When students have little opportunity to communicate about personal concerns as a part of ongoing learning activities, they become suspicious of occasional entrees into such areas. They tend to distance themselves from those whose questions come too close, with their resulting desire for space often being misinterpreted as unruliness or disrespect. To help students learn to communicate on a more intimate level with concerned adults, schools should establish an invitational climate, provide time for open discussions on contemporary issues, and encourage reflection. Teacher advisory programs are specifically designed to foster the personal and social development of pupils and should be considered when a school seeks to eliminate alienation. Chapter 7 discusses such a program.

The exemplary middle school is an educational institution in which the students are given the opportunity to establish or help determine the learning climate. Through interdisciplinary teams and teacher advisory programs, students are provided with opportunities to discuss and develop team rules and procedures. They in turn can have a say in the overall school procedures through representation on student council or other vehicles of representation. Such activities are means of fulfilling the school's responsibility to prepare young people for life in a democratic society.

A learner-centered school presents a cohesive, connected curriculum, one that fosters a total learning environment in schools and classrooms. Learner-centered programs and experiences enable learners to integrate all the parts of their educational experience into a whole. When students are able to do this, alienation is less likely to occur.

The socialization process, of course, is not the domain of the school alone but that of society as Callahan and Long (1983) explain:

> Socialization is the total process by which a nation reproduces itself through the conditioning of its young to merge with and extend society. It does not require financial support, trained personnel, or a particular institution to carry it on. Schooling takes place in an institution established to teach the young and is designed to accomplish pre-determined goals. — p. 19

In the past this socialization process has been the responsibility of the family, the church, and the community or neighborhood. This expectation has broken down in many instances, resulting in the school's becoming the logical setting in which to guide children through the socialization process. Today's teachers have had to teach courtesy as well as the causes of wars. Schools must encourage prosocial behavior while discouraging antisocial behavior. From preschool through high school, students should come to know why helping others is good from having experienced the role of a helper or engaging in service learning projects. Children need to see themselves as persons who are responsible and caring.

Too often schools promote prosocial behavior mainly by punishing antisocial behavior or by bribes – neither of which are effective means of changing behavior. Far preferable is for students to experience the satisfaction that comes when one does "good deeds" or helps another. Manipulation through extrinsic motivation reward systems offers children no reason to continue acting in the desired way when there is no longer any goody to be gained (Kohn, 1991). The use of extrinsic rewards for promoting certain kinds of behavior reduces the likelihood that students will perform those behaviors for their own sake. Prosocial behavior should be, and is, its own reward.

So many school practices are based on negative assumptions about kids that a shift in many of these assumptions will need to occur if the schools are to promote social behavior. Instruction will need to include training in cooperation, conflict resolution, and methods of achieving one's goals that do not require coercion or manipulation. Students say, and research studies confirm, that when they work together as a group they work harder, accomplish more and enjoy learning. Their socialization needs are being met while they pursue the academic goals.

Cooperative learning promotes prosocial behavior as children learn from one another. Its use creates a bond among those in the group while teaching cooperation. Students who work together generally feel good about themselves, about each other, about what they are doing; they actually learn more. The research supporting cooperative learning has more than demonstrated its value in raising student achievement, improving student social skills, enhancing student appreciation of human diversity, and strengthening student cooperation and collaboration (Poston, Stone, & Muther, 1992). This is a teaching strategy whose time has come.

Cooperative learning is the opposite of the more traditional approach in which each child works in isolation and competes against classmates. Children in school have been forced to work against each other or apart from one another and thereby develop the antisocial attitude of competitiveness. Opportunities to work with one another are left to chance and the students' own initiative for the most part. The socialization process should not be left to chance but carried out by the school in well designed efforts.

Cross-age tutoring or mentoring is another procedure that enhances socialization and builds self-esteem. For an older child to guide someone who is younger is to experience firsthand what it is to be a helper and to be responsible for someone who is dependent on another. Cross-age interaction for the younger student presents an opportunity to observe a prosocial model who is not an adult. Socialization comes from a synthesis of adult inculcation and peer interaction, and these values emphasize caring for others as well as applying principles of fairness (Kohn, 1991).

Prosocial behavior can also be taught through appropriate classroom management strategies. Classroom management can be like the learning process, one of cooperation and not one that assumes conflict. The topic of discipline provides a forum for problem solving and consensus. Involving the students in classroom management provides students with the opportunity to become responsible for their own actions and the actions of others. This fosters the concept of a community which is the purpose of socialization and demonstrates democracy.

Schools are like clubs in that one generation consciously tries to influence another – and in turn is influenced. For that to happen, both grownups and students have to see themselves as members of a common club.

Interdisciplinary teaming in middle schools helps to provide a club type atmosphere.

The school itself is a teacher, and its climate teaches much about socialization. The climate is determined by the people who work there, their attitudes about kids, the goals they have for themselves, and the processes used to pursue those goals. Everything that occurs in the school contributes to or distracts from a student's ability to achieve and be successful. Young people want to please adults and they want meaningful experiences. The environment has to provide an atmosphere that is conducive to student achievement and success.

Each teacher needs to create a nourishing environment, characterized by collegiality and fruitfulness. This can occur only to the extent that each teacher's own ethos mirrors these qualities. Adults who are secure themselves are able to provide a sense of security for young people. If teachers themselves are alienated and dissatisfied with their jobs, student alienation is sure to follow. In such cases strong efforts to help those teachers reassess their attitudes or to seek a transfer should be made. Usually teacher alienation can be reduced when supportive working conditions are in place, a sense of collegiality is fostered among the faculty, and the things that concern them are dealt with openly.

Children who are members of disenfranchised or alienated groups need to learn to use basic skills to help them understand and change their life circumstances. These youngsters must learn to hurdle the barriers they will face (such as discrimination), in order to make better lives for themselves within society (Sleeter & Grant, 1986). The structure of the school must provide for student individuality and not student conformity.

For the alienated, anti-social adolescent schools need to become caring and nurturing communities of learners. In order to do this, the school has to become one in which everyone knows everyone else as persons. Teaming provides this opportunity in larger school settings. The concept of "houses" does the same thing in large high schools. If an activity does not positively answer the inquiry "What kind of human relationship does this foster?" then it should be altered until it does.

The National Middle School Association (1995) in its position paper makes a case for a positive school climate in these statements:

> The climate of a developmentally responsive middle level school is safe, inviting, and caring; it promotes a sense of community and encourages learning....In a healthy school environ-

ment, human relationships are paramount, and individuals are treated with dignity and respect. Students and adults recognize and accept one another's differences; and curiosity, creativity, and diversity are celebrated. Issues of gender and equity are addressed with sensitivity and fairness. The climate encourages student risk taking, initiative, and building of substantive relationships.

— pp. 18-19

Education consists of a series of planned and unplanned experiences through which an individual learns how to live. The formal educational process, and to a large degree the informal one, is determined by the beliefs, aspirations, values, and influences of the culture with which the individual interacts. Thus, all children should have the opportunity to interact in an environment that confirms them as worthy human beings. The students need to feel that the significant others in their lives really care about what they do and how they feel. The effective teacher engages students in a warm and supporting manner. Interacting with others is important to enhancing further learning. Young adolescents are, by nature, curious; they want to explore and know how things work. Good schools and teachers capitalize on this curiosity and provide students with many opportunities for constructive experiences, time for reflective thinking, and a fail-safe environment in which they can be self-critical.

Constructivist learning is based on the belief that students construct new knowledge from the interaction of their existing knowledge with new ideas and experiences they encounter. The social constructivist believes that knowledge also has a social component and cannot be considered to be generated by an individual acting outside of the social context. Many of us learn best when we form study groups and engage in side conversations while studying.

In order for alienated students to connect to the school and view it as an extended family, the school environment must provide experiences that foster social and intellectual development. Dewey (1933) wrote, "Everything the teacher does as well as the manner in which he does it incites the child to respond in some way or another and each response tends to set the child's attitude in some way or another" (page. 59).

Students are often misjudged about what they are capable of learning. Adolescents like the "big questions" and yearn to pursue questions that adults believe are beyond their capabilities. Hopfenberg (1993) believes that a more challenging curriculum is more compelling to children, even so-called slow learners. This view is a tenet underlying some recent interventions such as the accelerated school.

The idea of providing extrinsic rewards for task achievement is not compatible with the broader definition of an education. A child has not truly learned a concept until it has been internalized. So the climate of the school has to be one that fosters internalization. A proper reward system should promote intrinsic motivation and internalization rather than achievement in order to receive a prize.

An integral aspect of one's education is learning that democratic communities have human qualities that are valued. Schools need to foster the development of emotional and social skills needed to live in a democratic society. This type of growth comes from the curriculum they encounter, the experience of interacting with their classmates, reflection on their experiences, and the relationships they developed while having those experiences.

The present school structure insists upon conformity and the teachers' rules and their standards have been used to maintain that conformity. Successful schools try to create a climate of membership for at-risk youth (Wehlage, Rutter, Smith, Lesko, & Fernandez, 1989). Membership depends upon social bonding – the extent to which an individual forms meaningful and satisfying links with a social group and the extent to which the group encourages the formation of those bonds. Social bonding has four elements: attachment, commitment, involvement, and belief (Arhar, 1992). Membership is not dependent upon conformity but upon social bonding.

Attachment refers to the social and emotional bonds to others, characterized by whether individuals care about what others think of them and their behavior. An individual will not care about others if he or she believes others do not care about him or her. The old adage "others don't care until you do" is certainly true with kids. Students who have a weak attachment to the school are likely to drift away and eventually drop out. Prosocial behavior has to be modeled and taught.

Commitment is part of bonding. It is the belief that remaining connected to a group is the rational thing to do to preserve ones' own self-interest. Without obvious short or long-term benefits, continued membership in a group is irrational. The school has to demonstrate some benefit to the student by offering short term goals and presenting avenues to long range benefits.

Involvement describes the extent of an individual's participation in the activities of the group or institution. Failure to be involved or withdrawing from participation often signals alienation. Schools must offer a strong co-curricular program that is attractive to all students. Involvement in academic, recreational, and sports activities allows students the opportunity to socialize in a setting that the school officially sanctions. These provide students a sense of membership in the school.

Belief is faith in the institution or group's legitimacy, a feeling that the school is beneficial to the student and that the student's membership is beneficial to the school. It determines if a student believes the school will lead to his or her desired goal. Short term achievable goals for students should be available within the classroom and within the school setting. The student must also be given opportunities to contribute to the school or to an organization within the school.

Young adolescents interact with their school environment by developing relationships with peers, teachers, and the school itself. Educators can enhance student social bonds to school by strengthening positive bonds within those three relationships. Strategies involve adults influencing student associations within the school, student associations with school peers, and student attachment to the school as an institution.

Adolescents want adult support and approval. Membership is based on a reciprocal process in which the faculty and the students exchange commitments. Bonding can be promoted by:

- Establishing mentoring relationships
- Creating small communities of support
- Making a commitment to all students regardless of background.

Membership requires that students have frequent and high-quality interaction with adults to reduce the sense of isolation. Students and teachers must view themselves as partners in the teaching/learning process. Within each classroom enough trust and openness must exist to encourage the sharing of ideas, the picking of brains, and constructive disagreement. The classroom social climate should help each student develop the requisite skills and attitudes for effective cooperation. People living in a society live most satisfactorily by cooperating.

Schools must integrate students into the life of the school so both the students and the school are mutually affected. Strategies that encourage linkages between the students and the school are:

- Make school rules explicit, fair, and equitable; apply them consistently.
- Base discipline on social contracts.
- Give students some control over their environment.
- Socialize students into the school during the elementary grades

Maynard (1977) states that rigid rules which apply equally to all students regardless of the circumstances, deprive teachers, counselors, and administrators the opportunity to teach behavior. Force will be met by force when the decisions have been made and there are few exceptions. There should be rules but they should be determined by students and staff, as well as by the administrators. They must also be fair and reasonable. Students must believe that they make a contribution to the system. Students respond more favorably to interpersonal contacts with adults than to impersonal rules and regulations. Helping students make informed choices is a discipline strategy that many schools use to give students a sense of personal control over themselves and their environments – cooperative discipline.

By interacting with peers, adolescents can distinguish themselves from those around them while developing a sense of social responsibility that goes beyond their own individual need for self-esteem. School is where adolescents seek social relationships with peers. Strong peer bonds develop as students participate in co-curricular activities, socialize with new students, and engage in peer mentoring programs

Studies of schooling and research from psychology and sociology suggest the importance of five factors to enhance student engagement in school: students' need for competence, extrinsic rewards, intrinsic interest, social support, and sense of ownership (Newman, 1989).

The impediments to membership include:
- Difficulty coping with school norms;
- Incongruence between home/community and school;
- Isolation of students from the mainstream of school activity; and
- Maladjustment to the large, impersonal social setting of many schools.

Principals must foster an atmosphere of support for both students and teachers; they must let students know that in school they will experience a familial closeness and concern for each other. The teachers should also know this.

Incongruence describes the personal and social mismatch between student and school. For students from lower socioeconomic status and racially and ethnically diverse backgrounds, the feeling that they do not fit into a middle class school can create a perception of self that is out of synch with the goals and values of the school. Incongruence is a major contributing factor to alienation.

Leaders can set a tone for the school by reducing the dominance of peer sub-groups such as "jocks" and "tough guys." They need to be replaced with a commitment to providing all students with in-depth, practical, and relevant educational experiences by a few adults who get to know student strengths and weaknesses. This commitment enhances the social bonding process.

## Conclusion

Many of our students are not comfortable when they arrive at school. Families and society place them in this position for many different reasons. Instead of contributing to the alienation factors, schools should be in the business of removing them or offering to counterbalance them.

School, to a child or a young adolescent, can be a very frightening place just because of size. Adults in the larger world have places of smaller size in which they feel secure and comfortable: families, church, clubs, or the workplace. Schools should be places of comfort and security.

Perhaps the surest way to find out what causes students to feel unwanted, unloved, or alienated by the school is to ask them. The greatest resource for answering questions about how to help students are the students themselves. They will tell us, and while their answers may not be what educators want to hear, the answers are what school people need to hear and act upon. ▪

# 4.
# Student/School
# Orientation

*I never met a man I didn't like.*
— Will Rogers

Entering into a new situation is always a bit scary. We are all somewhat frightened by the unknown, and even the most confident among us have some anxiety when moving into a strange environment. Remember the last visit to the hospital or clinic for tests, securing a loan, or joining a new church? They all caused some stress. Children undergo these same feelings when they move to a new school.

Wehlage et al. (1989) use the concept of membership in the school as another way of describing "engagement." They provide the following practices as necessary elements in the creation of school membership:

- Active efforts to create positive and respectful relations between adults and students;
- Communications of concern about and direct help to individuals with their personal problems;
- Active help in meeting institutional standards of success and competence;
- Active help in identifying a student's place in society based on a link between self, school, and one's future. — p. 154

Students returning to the school they attended last year have some anxiety as they anticipate new teachers and rooms and wonder who will be their classmates, when they will eat lunch, etc. If the idea of attending a different school is added, the anxiety for some students becomes almost intolerable.

A solid school orientation program for incoming students is essential if they are going to succeed, become connected, feel ownership, and believe that the school cares about them. Satisfying these goals for the students will ensure their parents/guardians will have the same feelings about the school.

An orientation program can be likened to a courtship and marriage. There is an introduction, a period of getting to know each other, growing acceptance, and finally a marriage. Unfortunately, neither the student nor the school chooses its partner, so the school must convince the student that he/she will be successful and happy at the school. Failure to do so places the young person in a precarious position before classes even begin.

### The Initial Orientation Meeting

A model orientation program begins in January or February with a PTA-sponsored meeting for all the parents/guardians of students who will be attending the school in the fall. These adults should receive a personal invitation from the principal and the PTA president. The elementary school teachers should encourage their students to attend the meeting. In schools that do this, approximately 90 percent of the parents attend.

After the obligatory welcome and introductions by the principal and PTA president, a video can be shown depicting the daily life and routines of students at school. Key personnel can be highlighted including the secretarial staff, nurse, counselors, administrators, head custodian, and cafeteria manager. The video shows students in the academic and exploratory courses, in physical education, and in after-school activities. It also explains special programs for the gifted or special needs child, the student advisory program, as well as student organizations such as student council and honor society.

After the video, the adults can be given an explanation of any course selection procedures that they, with their child, may need to complete. An adult and the child must sign the form and return it to the elementary teacher that week. The parents/guardians are also informed that a student may not have his/her schedule changed without the parent's involvement. While this last part is not necessary, it is a small way that the school can begin to build a partnership with the parents, establish credibility, and create trust with the parent. Necessary conditions!

Parents and students can be given handbooks and brochures such as NMSA's (1995) *What Is A Middle School?* These items provide information about the nature of middle level students. The information should also point out the differences between the middle level school and the elementary school and why those differences exist.

The booklet would explain the student advisory program if one exists, parental conference procedures, teaming, grading and reporting practices, testing programs, special education programs, and suggest ways parents can support their child and the school program. Parents are encouraged to keep these materials for future reference.

A detailed explanation of courses may be given now or held for later distribution. Course overviews provide the basic information that both parent/guardian and child need as they envision the year ahead. Sharing this information is another step toward establishing an open relationship between school and home.

Most parents are willing to trust the school and its staff in matters directly related to academics. It is in other matters connected with the schools that parents are more likely to be apprehensive. These are areas that they know something about and often, in their opinion, have more to do with their child's adjustment to school than do the courses themselves. These include:

- clubs, intramurals, socials, student council, honor society, and other activities;
- homework assignments;
- books;
- the calendar of school events;
- deliveries and messages to students (forgotten lunches, gym clothes, etc.);
- counseling services;
- health services;
- help sessions;
- library usage;
- lockers;
- lost and found;
- lunch/cafeteria;
- school store;
- use of vending machines;
- student use of telephones;
- use of bicycles, skateboards, and skates;
- bus conduct and safety;
- student discipline.

All of the above items can be explained in the parent handbook along with a section on study skill hints for parents/guardians. School board policies applicable to any of the above services may also be distributed. These policies provide the family members with essential information should the child receive discipline at the school or face other complications. Once again the parents/guardians see that the school is very willing to share information with them and not surprise them at some later date.

The student behavior issue should be addressed at length. Families and students need the assurance that violence and intimidation will not be tolerated. Scheduling a panel of students and parents of former students to field questions from the audience allows families to hear that the school provides a safe, caring atmosphere free of violence.

Each parent or guardian should receive a copy of the student folder. While the student folder contains information that is directly related to the student's daily routine and is written specifically for the student, it also contains information that parents may wish to know and discuss with their child. Often parents question when their child knew about a particular rule or if he/she was aware of a particular opportunity. Distributing the folder places the school in a defensible position and furthers the feeling of trust and openness.

After the parents have been given an overview of the handouts, each staff member with whom they may wish to speak should be introduced. These faculty members should include the team leaders and/or department chairs, counselors, special teachers, the nurse, sponsors of student activities, and officers of various student groups.

The staff should wear name tags and be available during the reception time following the meeting so parents/guardians can talk with them informally. Refreshments help to create an atmosphere in which parents can get to know school personnel on a one-to-one basis and voice any concerns and apprehensions.

### Visits to Feeder Schools

The next step in the process of easing the transition to a middle level school occurs a few weeks after the initial meeting when an administrator and a counselor visit each feeder school. Each would go to appropriate classes and answer students' questions about the school, its programs, activities, and any other concern. These visits provide the students with the opportunity to get to know the counselors and administrators, to see them as caring persons. This relationship is important to establish because the student needs to believe there will be an adult available in the fall with whom he/she can relate.

Each elementary student should receive a copy of the student folder as well as a small booklet entitled "Answers You Need," which could be prepared every year by the middle school's student council. Student council members are in a good position to provide incoming students with answers to questions they had when they started at the school. Using language students can identify with and enhanced with computer graphics, this booklet can be a very valuable item. Sometimes fifth graders write letters to sixth graders with their feelings and concerns. Sixth graders respond individually and become something of a buddy. In both cases the letter writing is an excellent language arts activity.

## Spring School Visits

The incoming students then visit the school in the spring. This visit should include lunch so they can experience how the cafeteria operates and observe the kind of behavior expected in the lunch room. Student council members give groups a tour of the school and brief visits in a few classrooms. After the tour is conducted these elementary students will have questions to ask, and they should be encouraged to do so. Both middle school staff and middle school students should be available to respond to the concerns of the visitors.

## Registration

The formal registration of students usually occurs in August. While a necessary and somewhat routine function, it does provide another opportunity to orient students, further ease their anxieties, promote the school's image, and to build a partnership feeling with parents and students. Every contact with any school personnel should lessen the student's anxiety and affirm to the family that the school is a safe place in which education is the primary function. Good organization and good human relationships give parents and students themselves the feeling that these educators know what they're doing.

As part of the registration process students and parents are given a chance to tour the school, locate rooms on the student's schedule, talk informally with school personnel, and generally become comfortable in the building. Students who have been in the summer transition program (described in a later chapter) or are student council members are stationed throughout the building to answer questions and serve as guides.

## PTA Reception

A PTA-sponsored reception during the first month of school is a standard practice in most schools. It provides another opportunity for parents/guardians and other family members to visit the school and learn more about it now that school is underway. Family members could meet with the appropriate team to discuss courses and the opportunities afforded children in the core subjects. Equally important is the opportunity to meet exploratory teachers and activity sponsors. This reception, usually well attended, is meaningful to family members since their children have already given them their perceptions about the school. This special evening may consume two or three hours, but its impact may last the whole time the child and parents are associated with the school.

## Lunch for Parents of New Students

During September all parents/guardians who have a child new to the school should be invited to have lunch with the student's team of teachers. One day a week could be set aside for this and be conducted weekly until all parents have been included. Adults buy their lunch from the same menu as the students. Tables are usually reserved for them, but they eat at the same time as their child and observe the cafeteria's procedures. The degree of socialization among the students is always an interesting things for parents to view.

Following lunch the visitors gather in the library for questions followed by classroom visits. Students are accustomed to having adults in the building and will not be intimidated by their presence.

## The Open House

In October the traditional school open house is held and is the final step in the formal process of orientation. Parents follow their student's schedule on an abbreviated basis, sitting in their child's desk, meeting each teacher and/or team in the appropriate room, and examining the instructional materials present. This event is essential because it gives family members a real feel for how their child spends the day; they can visualize what the school must be like during a school day. This activity, when combined with all of the other efforts, comprises a comprehensive program and gives parents a good perspective on the school.

## Conclusion

The transition from a neighborhood elementary school to a somewhat distant middle school is bound to be a source of some anxiety for both students and their families. Each school must understand the problems that early adolescents face when entering a new environment and alleviate those problems.

A comprehensive orientation program makes the transition process smooth and positive. The early efforts pay off in the long run. A transition program, if it is to help children, must also benefit the families.

A drag race program once included the slogan, "Every effort is made to ensure that each entry has an equal chance at victory." A well-planned transition or orientation program will go a long way toward making that slogan a reality in the school. The cost and time in relation to the benefit such a program yields are minimal. Any school can have a multi-faceted program and thereby reduce one aspect of schooling that puts many students at risk. It is logical to conclude that as stressful conditions are alleviated, the learning of individuals will increase.

Although not dealt with here, a transition program to orient eighth graders to the high school should be conducted in conjunction with the high school. The steps followed would be essentially the same. ∎

# 5.
# Summer
# Transition Program

*Yet it is honor I wish for them, honor and pride of person, not wealth.*

— Louis L'Amour

Each fall teachers identify students who are having difficulty making the transition to a new school. These students are not adjusting academically, behaviorally, emotionally, psychologically, or socially. Usually this identification occurs by the fourth or fifth week of school. It is a good news-bad news situation. It is good that students' problems are being recognized, but it is unfortunate that school is well under way before the problems are recognized.

Students who are likely to exhibit problems in their new schools need to be identified before the second month of school. Schools should be about the business of preventing these problems as well as providing programs for students after they are recognized as being at risk. Instituting a summer transition program prior to the start of school is one excellent way to prevent identified children from experiencing problems after the school year begins.

In this type of program the socialization aspect of the experience helps to reduce factors that create alienation. Kohn (1991) points out that helpfulness and responsibility ought not to be taught in a vacuum but in the context of a community of people who learn and play and make decisions together; the idea is not just to internalize good values in a community but to internalize the value of community. Everything is connected to everything else. In a summer transition program a sense of community can be achieved.

How do you identify those students who are likely to have academic difficulty in making the transition from an elementary school to a middle school or from a middle school to a senior high school? The staff of the receiving school would be hard pressed to do this. The feeder schools' personnel have to recommend those students who may have difficulty in making the transition. The faculty of sending schools are trusted in recommending students for other programs. Their judgments must likewise be trusted for selecting students to attend the summer transition program. In early spring, the principals, counselors, and teachers of the elementary schools can be asked to nominate students for the transition program.

Transition programs may include the typical at-risk child who exhibits almost all of the at-risk conditions or a child who may not have any of them. Every student has the potential of experiencing a temporary or even a permanent disconnection from productive learning in school. Many students do not fit the characteristics of at-risk students, but they may be ones who would have difficulty in moving from a self-contained classroom to a six-or seven-period day with six or seven different teachers each day. Factors to be considered when making recommendations include:

- retained at least once
- poor home environment/dysfunctional family
- evidence of poor peer relationships
- very introverted
- a history of being a troublemaker
- slow learner
- rebellious attitude.

Every child recommended will benefit from some part of the program if not all of it. Elementary teachers do a fine job in targeting students, but convincing some parents that the program is right for their child will be one of the more difficult tasks for the staff.

Summer transition programs have been very successful. Parents observe and experience personally something of the impact the program has on their children. Consequently it will be the topic of many conversations in the neighborhoods. When parents seek a worthwhile activity for their children in August, they will likely think of the transition program. Another type of transition program for students not recommended for the at-risk program might well be considered. Here the focus would be on enrichment or exploratory type activities rather than on catching up academically.

Any transition program should focus on self-esteem and student attitudes, because it is known that low self-esteem is correlated with school failure. The staff should make it evident that the school genuinely cares about the students and believes in their potential. A major goal should be to develop attitudes that would lead students to assume responsibility for their decisions, behavior, and learning. Success in school, as it is in life, is closely related to a positive attitude.

A good nucleus for a transitional program is the well-established Lions-Quest Skills for Adolescence Program (1988). This program has two main goals:

1. To help young people develop positive social behaviors, such as self-discipline, responsibility, good judgment, and the ability to get along with others.

2. To help young people develop strong commitments to their families, schools, positive peers, and communities, including a commitment to lead healthy, drug-free lives. — p. R-4

The Quest Program is a conceptual model that integrates theoretical approaches and research from several related disciplines. In three days of training, adult participants are taught how to teach skills and establish environments in order to meet the above goals. Other components of the transition program might include field trips, low-ropes, study skills, and orienteering. Each school faculty would need to analyze its resources and determine how they might best be utilized.

Several planning sessions would need to be held prior to the end of school and then again before the first parent meeting and the arrival of students. In addition to a coordinator, one teacher for every ten children is recommended. The program usually lasts 10 days. The hours and days are flexible from year to year so that proper use of resources may be meshed with the children's needs and the staff's training and capabilities.

The first day the students receive an overview of the program, engage in get-acquainted exercises, become familiar with the facilities, and meet the staff. An effective activity in the first session is a panel presentation that includes a member of the school board, a parent who has students in the school, a former student who has had success in high school as an athlete, a high school student who is active in school politics, and a former dropout who has gotten his act together. Students are encouraged to ask the panel any questions they wish about what it takes to be a success in school and secure a good education. By observing students during their interaction with the panel, the staff will gain insights into the students' behaviors, noting, for instance, those who withdraw and avoid eye contact, those who are upset by a particular question or an answer, and those who misbehave to get attention.

Another area deserving attention in the program is adolescence itself. The students can meet in large and small discussion groups to consider the social, emotional, physical, and psychological changes that puberty presents. They should be encouraged to be frank, open, and to share these discussions with their parents. A concerted effort to open parent/student communications should be a part of any program. Membership in the small groups should change regularly so that everyone will have a chance to interact with everyone else. This is very important so that when school starts, each student will then have a good chance of having someone in class that they already know. A sense of belonging and a group feeling of "we're special" results from the staff's efforts to make the program kid-centered.

The students can be divided into two groups for the next two days. One group goes through a low-ropes program at a local county park while the other group takes orienteering at a different site. On the following day the two groups switch activities. The low-ropes course is an outdoor challenge activity designed to teach students the value of good decision making, teamwork, and cooperation. Some of the learning outcomes of the low-ropes experience are that no one can succeed without help and teamwork, that each person has something to contribute in a challenging situation, and that everyone can't be successful at everything. Students, in general, love this type of activity.

The first orienteering activity may be conducted in the school so that the students can become familiar with the building and learn how to take directions. In order to be successful in school, students must learn how to follow directions, and orienteering is a great vehicle for this lesson. Later in the day these students can be taken to a city park where they can be given another orienteering exercise using compasses and maps. Again they will learn to be self-reliant, to depend upon each other, to follow directions, and to make good decisions.

On other days the activities may be designed to facilitate communications, decision making, problem solving, and personal responsibility. The sessions may have such provocative titles as *Celebrating the One and Only You, Taking Responsibility – You Are in the Driver's Seat, The Pits and the*

*Peaks, Pressure: Inside and Out, A Three-Step Process for Saying 'No,'* and *Building Bridges, Not Walls: Handling Conflicts in Friendships.*

A field trip relating to local history fosters community pride. The experience provides the students with insights into how the local area was settled and the role that the region played in the history of the country. A field trip with related activities also helps the youngsters realize that individuals can accomplish many things when they work in harmony.

An excellent culminating activity for students is a student-planned community service project that can be continued during the upcoming school year. Some possibilities are:

- Serving as aides at a senior citizen home;
- Starting paper re-cycling at the school;
- Building a compost pile for our school;
- Helping to beautify and maintain our campus.

The students who participated in the transition program should be monitored after school begins to be sure the gains made in the summer are maintained. Some of the students could be channeled into a peer helpers club where they can receive academic and emotional support. All should receive support and encouragement through the advisory program, and many may be helped further through involvement in clubs and intramural sports. Others may have to be pushed to become involved, and different avenues must be explored to ensure that all become engaged in some activity. Membership in a service organization is a possibility. Activities for such a group might include making posters for student registration, serving as building guides at school functions, cleaning up the campus, visiting senior citizens homes, making favors for teachers, and folding brochures for PTA meetings.

Every transition program should include a parental component. Four parent meetings are recommended. One would be held in June or July to familiarize the parents with the activities and the calendar of events, and to meet the staff. At this meeting the parents often will realize that the problems their children have are not unique. The other three meetings come at the start of the student activities, at the end of the program, and during the first month of school. At the first parent meeting it usually becomes apparent that parents are not aware of the tremendous physiological and emotional changes their children are going through during early adolescence. As they share information and discuss their problems, the family members often begin to function as a support group that communicates to students their interest and concern in school. Kids want to please their parents, and parental involvement leads to student success in school.

### Evaluating the Transition Program

To evaluate the transition program, the staff might use those students who were invited and recommended for the program but did not attend as a control group, the assumption being that the "no-shows" were as much in need of the program as those who attended. There is no objective way to measure degrees of need, so it cannot be stated with certainty that the transition program participants and the control group are comparable in all respects. Nevertheless, it does seem reasonable that comparisons between the two groups would provide some indication of the program's success.

Attendance rates, grades, and discipline referrals can be charted. Teachers' judgments are also valuable sources of data. Interviews with participants later in the school year provide particularly interesting and informative conclusions.

The cost of the program depends upon available resources in the community and local compensation policies for the staff. Costs may be offset by contributions from local businesses and manufacturers, donations, grants, and small fees paid by the participants. Creativity and initiative are key conditions for success in this and other aspects of the program.

To measure objectively the success of such a program is not possible. How can you measure the degree of improvement in self-esteem, self-discipline, or good decision making? Perhaps just the certainty that a summer transition program can't be detrimental and if it keeps one child from being unsuccessful in the new year, then it is worth the effort. ▪

# 6.
# Programs for
# Parents/Guardians

*Unfortunately, economic and social fac-*
*tors have seriously eroded the integrity and*
*functioning of the American family.*
— Martin H. Gerry and
Nicholas J. Certo

Parents are a child's first teachers and remain teachers and advisors into adulthood. Their attitudes about school and education have tremendous impact and greatly influence how well the child does in school. To build or maintain a child's positive attitude toward school and education itself, the family's influence must be channeled in that direction. There should not be any incongruence between the school and the home where the child's education is concerned. The basic premise is that if we are genuine, caring, empathic, and congruent as teachers, parents, or counselors, we will foster the growth and learning of others.

If there is a gap between the kinds of behavior rewarded in school and the norms and values of the homes and communities the school serves, students are likely to become alienated from school. To be alienated or marginal is to experience a strained, difficult relationship with the educational institution that has been organized to promote learning. Over time, this unproductive relationship with the school will limit the student's future opportunities and educational options. The school environment, of course, is both a factor that contributes to students becoming marginal and a resource for correcting that marginal behavior.

When the social network and style of the school are too dissonant from those of the home and neighborhood, the family's alienation from the school is communicated to the children When the perception that school is the enemy exists, it can effectively destroy the chances that a student will ever be successful in school. Schools need to inform parents about the nature and needs of early adolescents, enlist their active support, and then show how the school's programs accommodate those needs.

What do parents want from the school? Comer (1988) claims they want three things: First, they want to know what is going on in the school and how their child is doing. Second, they want to know how the system works and how they can be a part of it. Third, they want to know what they can do at home to help their child achieve in school (pp. 9-14).

Garvin (1988) based on extensive interviews with parents, came up with these factors in order of priority:

1. When their child goes to school, parents want to know that he or she is safe, especially about things like the bus, changing classes, the cafeteria, and free time. They want to be assured that their youngsters will feel safe and be safe throughout the day.

2. Parents want their child to know at least one adult to approach when problems develop and have that adult know the child well enough to be of help with those problems.

3. Parents expect the school to see that constructive interpersonal relationships are emphasized.

4. Parents associate their children's happiness with the degree to which youngsters feel they belong to the total school program.

5. They want their youngster to have successful experience each day to reinforce their good feelings about returning the next day.

6. Parents want their children to be challenged academically and to achieve, but they want learning goals to be realistic.

7. They want teachers to keep their children informed about their progress, and they seek opportunities to work in concert on problems. They especially want to know their role in homework.

8. They want to feel welcomed at the school, known by their names, and invited for more than just parent conferences.

9. They want school to help them learn more about what youngsters are like at this time, providing seminars, support groups, and access to resources and professional organizations. — pp. 55-56

There are many ways in which schools and homes can connect for the benefit of children and there are many ways to describe these connections. Epstein and Connors (1992) organized six types or levels of school/family interaction.

### Type 1. Basic obligations to families

Schools must provide families with information about adolescent health and safety, supervision, nutrition, discipline and guidance, parenting skills, and parenting approaches.

### Type 2. Basic obligations of school

Communications from schools to families about school programs and student progress.

### Type 3. Involvement at school

Schools increase the number of families who come to the school building by varying schedules so that more can participate as volunteers or serve as audiences at different times of the day and evening.

### Type 4. Involvement in home learning

Teachers must guide parents in monitoring, assisting, and interacting with their children at home on learning activities that are coordinated with class work or that contribute to success in school.

### Type 5. Involvement in decision making, governance, and advocacy

Parents and others in the community should hold participatory roles in parent-teacher-student organizations, school advisory councils, school site improvement teams, Chapter 1, and other school committees.

### Type 6. Collaboration and exchanges with the community

Schools, families, and students must establish connections with agencies, businesses, cultural groups, and community organizations that share responsibility for young people's education and their future successes.

— pp. 2-3

Schools must think through their plans for the type of family involvement they need and want. One good approach to planning is offered by Fantini (1986) who suggests a typology of parental approaches:

A. Parents as clients (participation as a privilege, public relations emphasis);

B. Parents as producers (parental support as volunteers in various supporting activities);

C. Parents as consumers (direct school services to parents on evenings/weekends);

D. Parents as governors (participation in evaluation, accountability, decision-making areas). — pp. 56-58

Increased parental involvement pays off. Evaluations of existing programs reveal that parents do help improve achievement, reduce absenteeism, improve student behavior, restore confidence and participation among parents, and participate more in children's learning development (McLaughlin, 1988). Henderson (1988) found similar results when parents/guardians are involved with their children's school. There is clear evidence that a family's concern for education, regardless of the educational attainment of a parent/guardian, is important to the student's success. And the more far-reaching the adult involvement, the more roles there are for family members to play in a school (Schorr & Schorr, 1988).

A true partnership between the school and home, the teachers and the family is a must. To achieve a viable partnership, Henderson, Marburger, & Ooms (1986) offer the following principles:

- Every aspect of the school should be "open, helpful, and friendly."
- Communications with parents should be "frequent, clear, two-way."
- Parents should be "treated as collaborators in the educational process, with a strong complementary role to play in their children's school learning and behavior."
- Parents should be encouraged to comment on school policies and, in some cases, "to share in the decision making."
- The school should recognize its responsibility "to forge a partnership with all families in the school."
- The principal and administrators should "actively express and promote the philosophy of partnership with all families."
- The school should encourage "volunteer participation from parents and the community-at-large." — pp. 27-31

Should schools allocate limited resources to recruiting parental involvement, offering parenting programs, and supporting homes in the rearing of children? Given the realities surrounding our youth today, the answer is certainly affirmative. Less than 10 percent of today's school children come from two-parent families with a single wage earner. Hodgkinson (1986) has characterized school children of the late 20th century in these statistics:

- 14% are born to unwed mothers
- 40% will have lived with a single parent by the time they reach age 18
- 30% are latchkey children

- 20% live in poverty
- 15% speak a native language other than English
- 15% have physical or mental handicaps
- 10% have poorly educated parents. — pp. 6-11

Cooley (1993) has listed many problems that impact on schools:
- One of every two marriages occurring since the early 1970s generally ends in divorce.
- 24 percent of youngsters under 18 currently live with one parent.
- Nearly 70 percent of youngsters in a single parent situation live with the mother.
- 51 percent of women returning to the labor force before their child reaches the age of one.
- Nearly 16 percent of children live in a stepfamily.
- Suicide is the second largest killer among persons 14-25.
- 21.9 percent of the class of 1988 indicated they first used alcohol in grades 7 or 8.
- 24 percent of students used marijuana prior to high school and 23 percent during high school.
- The United States leads all developed countries in teenage births and abortions.
- 56 million American families indicated alcohol-related problems, with incidents of child abuse reported by 41 percent of the families.
- 30 to 40 percent of females and 9 to 11 percent of males have been sexually abused by the age of 18.
- The rate of serious crimes has increased 11,000 percent since 1950.
— pp. 10-11

Why aren't parents more involved with their child's education? An inordinate proportion of those children living with single parents are also low achievers. Thus, one might deduce that a single parent has neither the time nor energy to be involved with the schools and their child's education. Parenting takes a lot of both. Parents must attend to domestic chores after work. If the child watches television and therefore takes none of the parents limited time and energy, so be it. If he says he has done his school work, so be it. The parent may be concerned about the education of the child, but active participation takes energy and time, both of which are limited for single parents. As the only ones available during the time of school functions, single parents may not be able to attend meetings.

Even two-parent families experience many of the same problems. As early as 1984 Campbell and Flake reported that 65 percent of the mothers of school-age children are in the labor force. This figure is now even higher. Many of these parents, thus, have the same energy and time limitations as do single parents. If one of the parents works nights, then that parent is a single parent as far as homework and attending school functions is concerned.

Although family structures have changed, Cole (1983) has taken the position that the responsibility of the home remains.

> Every home is a school, every parent a teacher. The existence of a formal system of schooling outside the home in no way absolves parents of their responsibility to guide and to teach. For better or for worse, children bear the indelible stamp of their upbringing long before they are mustered into the schools.
>
> If children learn the rudiments of reading, writing, and counting before they reach kindergarten, it's probably because of their parent's efforts. If they learn instead that time at home means time spent gazing blankly at the television, that too is a product of parental guidance or a lack of it. Learning begins at home.
>
> — p. 386

Psychologists are finding parallels between children of the urban rich and the urban poor. Both often suffer from broken homes and absentee parents; both have easy access to drugs, alcohol, and sex (Friedman, 1986). The problems of society touch all homes.

Manning (1985) has claimed that schools must have effective students and that behind effective students are effective parents. If parents do not have the time, energy, or know-how to be effective parents, how can educators expect effective students? Cole (1985) believes, "Educators have to step in to close the gaps that yawn between the haves and the have-nots" (p. 522).

Many parents do not accept the role of teacher eagerly or willingly. Some hold schools totally responsible for education while the home provides food, clothing, and shelter. Even when the schools offer to help, these parents resist. Unfortunately, those who stay away tend to be minorities, have less income and less facility with the English language, and are the only ones whose children are more often at risk of failing in school.

Generally, the public also seeks closer relations with the schools. Surveys show that most parents, regardless of their background, want guidance from the schools on ways to help their children learn better (Chavkin & Williams, 1989). Parents endorsed the idea of attending one evening a month to learn how to improve their children's academic performance.

A NIE survey (1988) of home-school programs in 24 large cities discovered the following kinds of activities that can help parents:

- Hotlines offering parents and students help with homework, school-related activities and problems, and social service referrals.
- District-wide parent-teacher conferences using attractive brochures and the media to alert parents, held in part during evening hours, and centered upon computerized testing information and suggestions for helping students at home.
- Parent training workshops based on student needs and parent interests such as how to help with homework, to tutor children at home, and to prepare them for minimum competency tests.
- Home visits to students and families with special needs for educational and social services, or to train parents in educational methods.
- Educational service teams composed of an educator, psychologist, and social worker who provide special help and guidance to students and also work with parents.
- Contracts parents sign agreeing to help their children prepare for schoolwork.
- Attendance monitoring by special staff and prompt contact with parent of absentee. — p. 5

Two very successful programs for incorporating all of the various factors of involving parents in school have been Unite for Success and Success for Surviving Adolescence described below.

### Unite for Success

At Hazelwood Junior High School the question was asked; Do we need more parent and community involvement? The answer was *yes*, because the parents already involved represented those homes that did support education and their children's learning efforts. Many of the single parents and the ones where both parents worked could not volunteer or attend parent functions and felt they could not be actively involved. This did not mean they were not interested in what the school was doing or their child's education. It meant that if the school was going to involve more parents, additional efforts were needed. Unite for Success became the vehicle for achieving this goal.

The Unite for Success committee established monthly themes to be shared with faculty, parents, and families. These themes corresponded with those established for PRIMETIME, the teacher advisory program. A set of suggestions, activities, and guidelines was mailed to each family.

Designed to create an atmosphere in which parents could be actively involved, families were also reminded about the "basics" for which they must be responsible. The faculty wanted them to know that teachers believe that families provide the key ingredients for children's successes. High expectations, positive attitudes about themselves, school, and life, good study habits, self-discipline, and motivation do not come from television, a textbook, or friends at the mall. These are family responsibilities. The school was there to assist, but it needed parental help to build the foundation.

The Unite for Success logo contains intersecting circles with a figure of a child in the overlapping portions. The child lives in both systems and both institutions are intertwined. A figure eight with the childlike figure at the intersection of the upper and lower halves would also have been appropriate. The monthly themes, the helpful hints, the activity suggestions, and the continuous school-to-home contacts impacted all families and encouraged involvement.

### Success for Surviving Adolescence

The 1996 Gallup/Phi Delta Kappa Poll of Teachers showed that teachers believed the parents' lack of interest and support was the biggest educational problem – not drugs, not weapons, not discipline, not tardies, but parental apathy. Yet, school districts have programs dealing with all of these, but there are none offered for parents. If schools offered parenting programs, then maybe those for drugs, weapons, discipline, and violence wouldn't be needed. Families need an opportunity to receive training on how to help their children within their limited time. Parents must know how important their help is in determining the success of their children's educational future. This line of thinking led to the creation of the program "Success for Surviving Adolescence."

"Success for Surviving Adolescence" features monthly meetings that utilize the themes developed for PRIMETIME and Unite for Success. The three programs must be correlated and mutually supportive, because parents, teachers, and students are closely interrelated.

All meetings follow the same format. They are one and one half hours long and held on the same evening each month. Parents are encouraged to make it a regular part of their lives just as they do a favorite TV show.

The format for a meeting is:

I.   Icebreaker
II.  Presentation of a concept or theme
III. Parenting skill
    a. Introduction
    b. Modeling of skill (role playing)
    c. Practice
IV. Open parent groups
    A. Questions and answers
    B. Support groups
    V. Refreshments - informal time.

For the theme of self-identification, the icebreaker was a people search in which each person had to find individuals who had one of the listed characteristics. This activity involved everyone and was a step toward forming support groups. A sense of community begins to develop with the icebreakers.

The topic of self-worth or self-esteem was presented by several teachers, a counselor, and the communication department chair. Its importance to students, why it is so fragile, and how it can be destroyed or built were aspects discussed. The parenting skill focused on how a child's self-esteem may be destroyed or enhanced through daily communications with adults. Parents were informed that words like *ought, should, must, dumb,* and *always* are detrimental to self-esteem. Words and attitudes that imply mutual respect, a feeling of confidence in the child, and love were avenues to building children's self-esteem and self-worth.

Teachers role-played a conversation between a child and a parent. The child had received a failing notice. Initially, the parent lambasted the child with self-esteem killing statements. Re-done, the parent used self-esteem building comments that still let the child know that he/she was unhappy about the grade. Parents/guardians were given a scenario to act out as they might normally behave, and then asked to change to a self-esteem enhancing mode. Many were impressed and dismayed by what they had been saying and encouraged by what they now realized they could say.

The session concluded with questions and answer. This was very effective since the previous activity brought to mind some recent conversations parents had had with their children. They wanted to know what should have been said. People do not willingly choose to put their children down but often do not know better.

## Conclusion

In January of 1991, President Bush in the State of the Union address admonished parents. "We've got to take the time after a busy day to sit down and read with our kids, help them with their homework, pass along the values we learned as kids. And that's how we sustain the 'state of the union'."

What if parents want to do right but do not have the skills? Then the school must take steps to teach those skills and connect family to the school. The traditional nuclear family no longer exists. Traditional relationships between schools and families therefore can no longer exist. Given the divorce rate, single-parent homes, homes where both parents work, the poverty rate, neighborhood dissolution, almost any child can come to school under stress. Some parents seldom confront the school, primarily because they have been socialized to accept the school's authority. One way to alter this situation is to train parents to be more assertive but still courteous.

In order to raise children, the family increasingly needs support and sustenance from the school and other community agencies. Children are alienated, families are dysfunctional, and if the educators do not offer and give assistance then schools also become at-risk. When families turn their considerable interpretive and screening powers to support and extend the social and academic priorities of schools, a compelling force for successful learning is in effect (Sinclair and Ghory, 1987).

Home atmospheres can be changed by assisting parents to be better parents, by teaching them how to work with children on learning activities at home. Unite for Success and Success for Surviving Adolescence are two programs that can assist in this important effort. $\blacksquare$

# 7.
# A Teacher
# Advisory Program

*A teacher effects eternity; he can
never tell where his influence stops.*
— Henry Brooke Adams

Helping students develop a sense of purpose, feel part of a nurturing community, and believe in themselves enough to make wise choices are keys to preventing adolescents from falling behind and becoming alienated. Given the state of our society, educators in individual schools need to take the initiative in seeking to develop the attitudes and self-esteem that will prevent young adolescents from dropping out – of school and life. Educating young people to assume active roles in a democracy is an important but difficult task. When that democracy does not provide a protecting, nurturing environment for many of its young, then that task is compounded and the school must broaden its mission to go beyond the transmission of knowledge.

Ideas, principles, values, and expectations are not taught by a teacher in the same manner as mathematics or music. They are concepts that must be felt, breathed, experienced, and lived if they are to influence young people. Since society in local communities seldom does this for all students, particularly in large urban areas, then the schools must develop a culture, a climate, and a close community so students can experience democratic values.

The problems that face many of our young people are overwhelming, at times catastrophic. Schools can help by providing close continuing contact between a student and an adult. Youngsters need someone to encourage, cheer, discipline, reward, prod, and at times even punish. Simply put, students need someone who listens and really cares about them.

When such a relationship between an individual student and a teacher develops, success in school is far more likely to follow.

A teacher advisory program is one way to engender the desired student-teacher relationships. *Turning Points* (1989), in noting that the middle school is the "last, best hope" for positively influencing students who are most likely to fall prey to high risk behaviors (estimated to be seven million children, with another seven million at moderate risk), recommends that middle schools create small communities where students and teachers have an opportunity to know each other well over time, particularly through teaming and small group advisories.

The middle level school of tomorrow will ensure extended guidance for all students. Facing many fateful decisions relative to sex, drugs, alcohol, as well as further educational opportunities and vocations, young adolescents need all the help that trained personnel can give them. In good middle schools, not only will knowledgeable teachers give guidance, but other specially trained counselors and school psychologists will be available to assist.

The National Middle School Association's position paper (1995) states:

All adults in developmentally responsive middle level schools are advocates for young adolescents. In addition, each student has one adult who knows and cares for that individual and who supports that student's academic and personal development. This designated advocate or advisor must be a model of good character and be knowledgeable about both young adolescent development and middle level education. — p. 16

The Council on Middle Level Education of NASSP (1985) recommended, "Institute student advisement programs that assure each student regular, compassionate, supportive counsel from a concerned adult about his or her academic programs, adjustment to school, and personal adjustment" (p. 4).

Advisory programs provide the young adolescent with regular opportunities for small group interaction with peers and a caring adult. The adult's role is not only as a caring and sympathetic person, a "friend," but also as one who can make referrals to the school counselors and other specialists when necessary. Though difficult to institute because teachers often feel unprepared to fulfill this role, when done well, adviser-advisee programs have proven to be very successful and well received.

In a successful advisory program students find a nonthreatening environment in which they are able to develop a sense of emotional well-being, explore developmental changes, improve social skills, consider career opportunities, analyze current events, and enhance their ability to achieve academic success. Advisory programs help students approach the highly significant goals of education: self-actualization and human dignity, as well as academic achievement.

Only after basic emotional and social needs have been met can real learning take place. The student advisory program is one way of helping students meet those needs and adjust to the changes that pervade their lives. The teacher/advisor becomes a "significant other" in the student's school life, an advocate, a friend from whom the student can seek advice and be assured of understanding. The advisory program offers a "home away from home" while at school. It is a constant for the student.

### An Example of an Advisory Program

A successful advisory program called PRIMETIME was developed by the faculty where the author was principal.

The specific goals of PRIMETIME are to provide the student with the opportunity to:

- Communicate and develop rapport with a teacher.
- Establish a positive relationship with a multi-age, small peer group.
- Strengthen the individual's self-concept.
- Develop social, problem solving, decision making, and communication skills.
- Develop pride in the school and community.
- Develop a widening range of personal, social, aesthetic, academic, and career interests.
- Develop school unity and school spirit.

While the program was developed to meet student needs and further their educational goals, parents also received benefits in these ways.

- Knowing that their children will have a caring adult in the school setting who knows the student well.
- Having a single person to contact concerning any school welfare problems.
- Developing a greater respect for teachers who serve in the role of advisor.

- Receiving fewer calls concerning discipline matters.
- . Recognizing that self-direction skills are a focus of the school program.
- Observing more positive attitudes in their child and fewer stress behaviors.
- . Knowing that the school is taking the initiative in efforts to ensure student success.
- Knowing that children are getting emotional, social, and academic support from both peer group and the professional staff.

Silent Sustained Reading is an effective activity for use in PRIMETIME. Students read quietly from material of their own choosing. (In some schools the program is labeled DEAR – Drop Everything And Read.). Having students read for twenty minutes encourages the habit of reading. For the young adolescent, reading during PRIMETIME is non-threatening, no grades are involved, just a chance to enhance a skill. Teachers also read uninterrupted.

Directed Study Period on another day of PRIMETIME provides students with time to complete homework assignments or work on projects. The teacher supplies study skills instruction and other assistance as conditions warrant. Early in the year, the advisor may use this period for review of some formal study skills, test taking tips, note taking, etc. To assist the student who may have difficulty in organizing, the following types of questions could be asked or put on the board:

- What subjects are you going to work on?
- Do you have the materials you need to complete the assignment?
- If you have more than one assignment, how will you divide your time?
- What conduct is expected of all of us so that every one can complete his/her assignments?

Current Events on another day lets students consider events both at school or in the outside world. The discussion of national and world events can be facilitated by asking: How will or might this event affect you or your family? What are some possible long-range consequences of this event? What is likely to happen next? Students are encouraged to keep up with current affairs by watching television and reading newspapers. In the event of major events, locally or nationally, any day in PRIMETIME can be a current events day.

Choice Day permits flexibility and creativity to promote personal growth, engage in physical activities, conferences, school-wide problem solving, and work on contest/competition endeavors. Many groups use this day for a community outreach activity.

The idea of Success Circles was developed to provide a time, place, and an agenda for meaningful interaction between caring adults and students to enhance the development of the students' social skills. Lessons designed to last the length of the advisory period provide expression for each teacher's personality and teaching style and are flexible enough to fit each advisory group. Retzer (1992) notes, "When a circle of friends sharing a mutual concern joins with other similar circles, a very large, very effective circle can be formed" (p. 5). This is what can result from a school-wide advisory program.

The planned but flexible curriculum for Success Circles was designed to fit in a file box to encourage the addition of ideas, materials, and resources. Within the box are dividers in the school colors. The tabs on these dividers spelled out SUCCEED. This word established the manner of organization, provided continuity, and kept the themes and time frames at the faculty's fingertips.

| | | |
|---|---|---|
| S - | Self-identifying (Sept/Oct) | introductions<br>identify adolescence<br>self-awareness |
| U - | Understanding (Nov/Dec) | interpersonal relationships<br>(family, friends, teachers)<br>social skills |
| C - | Communicating (Jan) | listening skills<br>visual/oral communication<br>perception of others |
| C - | Cooperating (Feb) | peer relationships<br>conflict resolution |
| E - | Emerging (Mar) | self-growth<br>values clarification<br>thinking processes and skills |
| E - | Exploring (April) | peer pressure<br>careers<br>long-term goals |
| D - | Decision making (May) | skills<br>problem solving |

Teachers approach the circle with their own instructional style. A teacher used to directing a teacher-centered classroom cannot be expected to start using an interactive group process immediately. Everyone had to feel comfortable about the process. As time went by and the activities themselves encouraged an informal student-centered room, teachers become more comfortable with and adept at directing the advisory program in a less directive manner.

The Wheel of Success was developed for teachers as they selected their activities for Success Circles. The wheel for the self-identifying theme was divided into six divisions of activities. Thus, for the three September Success Circles meetings, teachers had six activities from which to choose – twice as many as needed.

1.   String along with me
2.   Knowing yourself
3.   This makes me special
4    Getting to know you
5.   Achieving your goal
6.   Social skills inventory test

The next circle, toward the center, indicated the teaching style usually associated or identified with that activity. The five styles identified were:

A =   Active
W =   Written
L =   Lecture
D =   Discussion
G =   Group

The activity "Getting to know you" was a group-oriented process, but "knowing yourself" involved a written and discussion format. Both would help students with the theme of self-identification. The teachers picked the activity that best fit them and their preferred method of interacting with students.

Success Circles were not intended to make every teacher become a quasi-counselor. There is an old but true cliché that claims "Kids don't care how much you know until they know how much you care." In these activities the caring of teachers can be manifested. The faculty do not formally counsel kids, but they listen and share their understandings relative to:

- self-esteem
- responsibility
- self-control
- respect
- honesty
- reliability
- decision making
- commitment
- cooperation
- courage
- patience
- initiative
- discretion
- compassion
- kindness
- perseverance
- assertiveness
- goal setting
- time management
- problem solving

### Conclusion

Over the past three decades many schools have realized that it is in their best interest and that of their students to establish student advisory programs. Although difficult to organize and maintain, such programs serve kids who are at risk, kids who are "normal," kids who are "gifted," the kids who are "handicapped" – all kids – to help ensure their chance to succeed. PRIMETIME is one example of a program that made school a more pleasant place and helped to ensure that all students would be more successful in all aspects of their development. ⬛

*I find ways, I do what it takes. Sometimes I lose, but I persist. When I lose, I go down fighting.*

— Len DeAngelis

# 8.
# A Tutorial Program

Schools compete for students' time. Teachers vie for students' time within the schools, with other instructors, and with school activities, but other outside interests also bid for students' time. Students today have many activities available that interfere with their success in school. This reality, coupled with poor study habits and home environments that may not be conducive to studying, place many students at risk of failing.

When students who don't do their homework are asked why, they usually confess to watching TV. Studying requires skills, effort, and usually parental supervision. TV watching or listening to music requires no skills, little effort, and absolutely no supervision. A 1988 study sponsored by the U.S. Department of Education (1990) reported that a typical eighth grader spends four times as many hours watching television per week as on homework on school days, and about 25 percent report being home alone two or more hours a week without an adult present. Hood (1992) tells us:

> In reality many adolescents do not look forward to going home at the end of the school day. They suffer from stress and tension of knowing that home is not a comfortable place to be. They know that home is merely a roof, videos, and pizza. Home means being alone for hours until an adult walks through the door.
>
> And even then, home may still mean being alone. (p. 20-22)

The lack of parental supervision for young people is an ever-growing national concern. Most students need adult prompting to do their school work. Parents who work second or third shifts are just not available to their children during non-school hours. Commuting absorbs precious hours in the lives of a substantial number of parents. More and more students then have less and less adult supervision. When parents are at home, the duties of laundry, shopping, cooking, etc. take priority and distract from the parental responsibilities of seeing that the child completes homework. Fatigue too is a factor that takes its toll.

The lack of time for supervision comes at the very time when more emphasis is being placed on homework. Homework has long been and continues to be a staple of American education. If it is vital to the educational process and if it is not being completed at home, then does it not become the responsibility of the school? If it is, then schools should develop a program to assist with the completion of homework. A tutorial program may be planned to achieve this goal. In addition to supervising the completion of homework, a tutorial should focus on helping students develop study skills and provide individual assistance.

For classroom instruction to be effective, expectations must be high, standards clear, evaluations fair, and students held accountable for their efforts. While the tutorial program can assist with the marginal learner, it is also recognized that some students need more direction than others. Therefore, the program should take into account the wide range of motivation and maturity among students. The tutorial program also needs to send a clear message to parents that education is a shared responsibility and their involvement is vital to the success of their student and the program.

The program called the OK CLUB provided one hour tutorial sessions at the close of the school day. When a student was recommended to the OK CLUB either by a teacher or parent, or by self-referral, a form that called for pertinent information was completed by each core subject teacher. Copies of the OK CLUB form were sent to the guidance office, teachers, the student, and parents.

The tutorial sessions met Monday though Thursday with a maximum of ten students per teacher. Any one student attended two days a week but could request additional sessions if desired. A great deal of flexibility was permitted so that students could still participate in other after school activities and functions.

The teachers used and adapted materials from many excellent sources. Perhaps most important was the overall positive approach exhibited by teachers toward the program and the students. The OK CLUB reinforced the advisory program. When students begin to feel good about themselves, their studies, and their school, they are on the road to success. Building their self-esteem, coupled with work on study skills, helped these students, but there was a third component vital to the program's success – the parent program that was discussed in Chapter 4.

### Parent evaluation

When asked their impression of the OK CLUB, 388 parents responded favorably and 28 unfavorably. Some typical comments were;

*I think that it has helped my daughter, and it also has helped us.*
*My child is more aware of studying and doing homework.*
*It makes me feel that the school really wants my child to do well.*
*A positive effort to help children improve in school.*
*I think it is a fantastic program.*
*It fosters a positive relationship between the school and the home.*
*It was good to know that other kids and parents have problems.*

When asked what their child's impression of the OK CLUB was, parents responded with such statements as:

*Once he stopped thinking of it as punishment, I believe he enjoyed being a part of the group. He now knows he is not the only one with a problem.*

*He felt it was a punishment at first, then felt it a punishment again the last two weeks. However, he did admit it helped him.*

*At first he saw it as punishment, but gradually seemed to feel that he could get his work completed and have some positive help. It was a logical consequence that seemed to work.*

*He felt it was helpful, and he's glad he was involved in the program. He feels like he has learned some good study habits.*

*At first, not very responsive, but as time went on, his ideas changed.*

When asked whether the program was beneficial for their child, 70 percent of the parents said "yes," 10 percent said "no." Twenty percent were undecided. Some of the favorable comments were:

*Yes, I think it has taught my child better study habits. Before he was in OK CLUB, I had to help him get started on his homework. Now he can do a good part of it with no assistance,*
*Yes, I just hope it is a lasting one.*

*Yes, several small, but certainly noticeable, changes.*

*Yes, more efficient use of time. He has a plan of attack for his homework.*

*Yes, he seems to be striving hard as far as his study and work habits.*

Among the approximately 10 percent that were negative, such comments as these were typical:

*She viewed it as punishment.*

*He hated it.*

*His grades didn't get any better, and he didn't like it.*

## Teacher Evaluation

The teachers' evaluations were as supportive of the program as were those of the parents. They reported that the OK CLUB students were better prepared for class, more attentive, better organized, and in several instances, had a better attitude toward school and, more importantly, toward themselves. The teachers' evaluations indicated an increased appreciation for the teaching of study and organizational skills. They also expressed the value of parental involvement and reported noticeable improvement in those students whose parents had been conscientious about attending the parent meetings.

The faculty also noticed that students were not losing as many papers and were showing more concern for completing their homework. They also agreed that providing an environment conducive to study was a key to success for many of these students, since parents do not always monitor the quality of their children's homework nor provide the structure that this program offers.

## Student Evaluation

Although it was difficult to directly assess gains in self-concept, organizational skills, and accepting responsibility, these qualities were reflected indirectly in the grades OK CLUB students received in the four basic academic areas. Of the 1,240 grades given in a grading period, 39 percent showed improvement, 50.32 percent showed no change, and 10.68 percent declined. In terms of achievement in the four areas, 85 percent showed improvement in one area, 11 percent improved in all four areas, and 20 percent showed no improvement. While the program could not be judged a success for all students, it must be remembered for the most part that these were failing students; so if 30 percent of the total grades improved and if 85 percent of the grades improved in at least one area, then this was a significant improvement for this population. Perhaps many of the student grades that showed no improvement might have declined without OK CLUB.

## Conclusion

In light of subjective comments made by students, parents, and teachers together with the data on grades, the OK CLUB must be viewed as a success. While it may not have made a difference in the educational success of all students enrolled in the club, it was clearly an important factor for the large majority. Other schools should consider a comparable program if they want to ensure success for all students. $\blacksquare$

# 9.
# Individualized Course Alternative, Now or Never (I-CANN)

*Sometimes we look for too complex answers to problems, when a realistic, commonsense approach to improving self-image is the answer.* — Jackard

Alternative courses for those students who are not successful in the regular programs of the school are varied and many. The program described here could be adopted by any school and adapted to utilize available resources and conditions.

Most so-called at-risk students and dropouts do not have low intelligence. They have low self-esteem, are typically two years behind their peers in math and reading, and by the time they are in the seventh grade they have been retained at least once (DeBlois, 1989). These students tend to drive their teachers to distraction relative to academics, but are often quite friendly and do not always get visibly upset with their lot in school. They just cannot seem to cope in some subjects while in other activities they do quite well.

There is no easy answer for such students nor is there a ready explanation for their disruptive behavior and lack of achievement in some classes. When asked for an explanation they often shrug their shoulders and offer such comments as "I don't know," "I don't like the teacher," "I don't like the subject," "I don't have any of my friends in that class." A class with several of these students can be very frustrating. The youngsters have a variety of problems and often what the school does to help them makes their difficulties worse.

Students consider dropping out because they believe they are not going to succeed in school. Their high rate of absenteeism, lack of involvement in school, poor socialization skills, inadequate communication skills, and alienation factors all indicate their judgment is sound. Therefore the school must change those elements of structure and curriculum that have created the negative conditions and provide instead ones that offer opportunities for success.

Valencia (as cited in *Educating At-Risk Youth,* 1993) identifies the following components as being important in comprehensive programs for at-risk students:

1. An effective system for identifying at-risk children in the early school years.
2. Instructional strategies and arrangements that take into consideration the unique linguistic and cultural factors of minority students.
3. Appropriate assessment instruments and grading approaches which emphasize successful outcomes through constructive feedback and recycling.
4. A monitoring system to determine the progress of at-risk students, coupled with provision for immediate positive action that will encourage them to continue pursuing their education.
5. Academic remediation and tutoring; career counseling and goal setting; and counseling services for students with personal problems attributed to pregnancy, drug, alcohol and child abuse.
6. Alternative school arrangements to accommodate students with special educational needs.
7. Cooperative work-experience arrangements to enable at-risk students to complete high school while they gain employable skills through on-the-job training.
8. Collaborative arrangements between the high school and local college or university to encourage academically capable at-risk students to pursue post-secondary or university studies.
9. Inservice workshops for teachers, counselors, administrators, and other school personnel on strategies and procedures to develop and implement an effective program for at-risk students.

— p. 8

In describing the Shawnee Mission Alternative Education Program, which was specifically designed for the potential drop out, Jackard (1988) believes that essential to the success of the program is daily counseling, so that the staff and student can identify individual problems and then try to work on them. The way individuals feel about themselves governs the manner in which they deal with both problems and successes. Jackard goes on to offer the following synopsis of a philosophy that is conducive to developing a successful program for the at-risk student.

- Accept all people as worthy human beings, you don't have to accept what they say or do.
- Provide lots of tender loving care and genuine concern for all people.
- Develop a positive self-image and use a positive approach when dealing with people.
- Handle situations in a mature manner, never allowing other people to bring you down to their level.
- Observe patiently and objectively all interactions with people.
- Communicate effectively – make sure people understand what you expect and what the consequences will be.
- There is no single method that works with all people. Analyze the personality of the person you are dealing with and adapt your personality accordingly.
- Keep in mind that you are human too; therefore, you will make mistakes.
- Above all, treat other people as you would like to be treated.

— p. 128

The Individualized Course Alternative, Now or Never (I-CANN) was developed and implemented for students who "fall through the cracks." I-CANN was based on the assumption that all students have the capacity to learn more than the minimum requirements and that the school can be the place where their learning can begin.

Students were taken out of the subjects in which they were failing or in the classrooms where they were disruptive. Scheduled into a smaller group setting they were helped "to get their act together." Students came to see I-CANN as their program; one in which they could be themselves. They formed a strong informal support group and each one's problem became every one else's. Thus, counseling became an important component of the program, perhaps the most important component. I-CANN students received group and often individual counseling on a daily basis. They formed a close working relationship with the teacher and counselor. They engaged in hands-on cooperative activities, with each student contributing his/her skills to accomplish the task. The curriculum was essentially the one presented in the regular classes except it was developed around a series of meaningful projects. The class size, the relaxed atmosphere, and the treatment of students as worthy and capable all helped to create a climate that permitted them to learn both skills and content as they grow in stature in their own eyes and those of their peers.

Characteristics of a program like I-CANN should be: small settings with low student-teacher ratios, personalized attention to student needs, materials and teaching formats that stress immediate, practical emphasis on basic academic skills, student-initiated exploration, problem solving, consistent patterns of rewarding student achievement, and, in many cases, the capacity to service an English as a Second Language population. A vocational emphasis seems to be helpful.

"Who Am I" was an introductory project in the program that helped students understand themselves and others. The students developed collages using visuals that represented their likes, dislikes, interests, and attitudes. Upon completion, the students wrote a paper summarizing their work, and presented a videotaped interpretation of their collage. The students enjoyed this project and it was a very beneficial way for the teacher and counselor to learn more about each student. Producing the videotape seemed to boost self-esteem and self-image for the students.

One successful activity that provided problem-solving experiences and the application of basic skills was having the students actually set up a small business. Students learned trust, cooperation, and that hard work can be profitable. I-CANN Co, Inc. was the longest-running project undertaken and perhaps the most beneficial. The business involved many decision-making skills as the students considered what product might be manufactured, what materials would be needed, what they would cost, how they could produce it, and how could they sell it and for how much. This planning process developed teamwork and improved their socialization skills.

Each student prepared a resumé, secured references, and was interviewed by the teacher and the counselor for the jobs within the company. When the positions were filled and materials gathered, production was started. The companies manufactured key chains, calendars, memory books, bakery goods, and provided a tie-dye service. Products were sold to the student body, usually during lunch. The kinds of activities and projects may be varied. Students can research community laws, do surveys, study traffic patterns, conduct a census, interview senior citizens, construct scale maps, produce books, plays, videos, radio shows, and puppet shows, fly kites, and predict the future.

Perhaps the most important lesson learned was how their previous attitudes and work habits would affect their future employment prospects. Several were dismayed to find that there was no one they could ask to give them a good reference for a job. They began to understand that what they did now affected their future.

### Conclusion

An I-CANN type program could be developed in any school. A creative teacher, a caring counselor, a supportive principal, and students who need such a program are the ingredients needed. I-CANN was an alternative program for alienated students designed to prevent them from dropping out. The students grew closer to each other and to the staff, and they shared some very heavy problems.. They had an ear; they had a peer culture with which to relate; they had non-preaching adults to interact with; and they were learning! S

# 10.
# Time for Success:
# Putting it All Together

*An effective classroom climate is practically invisible, but it doesn't happen by chance; it is crafted by the artful teacher in subtle but intentional ways.* — Marzano

There is a wholeness to life; all things are connected and interrelated. Within a school there must be a consistent philosophy and all of the components and programs must work within and be compatible with that philosophy. All of the programs at the school where the author previously served as principal operated under the umbrella concept "Time for Success."

At a retreat, the faculty decided that the school could no longer function as it had in the past. While it had been a successful school in the past, the faculty realized that this guaranteed nothing for the future but a base upon which to build.

To be successful with students, the faculty had to influence what was occurring in the students' lives during the other eighteen hours a day and on the week-ends. This concept is fundamental to real reforms but is often overlooked. Too many of the students had concerns that overshadowed what teachers were trying to do in class. Too many of them came from families that could not or did not support their child's learning efforts. Others came from homes that wanted to help their child but did not know how. This, then, became the immediate goal – to establish programs that would ensure success for all students, involve families in the educational enterprise, influence students' behavior when not in school, and make it possible to meet the academic objectives of school.

The faculty wanted a school-wide approach and not a few isolated programs. Continuity and program congruence were uppermost in their minds. "Time for Success" became the umbrella under which all of the programs would operate. It was time for our students to experience success and it was time for our school to ensure that success.

"Time for Success" provided a label with which the faculty, students, parents, and the community could identify. It provided a focus, expressed an attitude, and gave us a slogan.

A clock face was chosen as the logo for "Time for Success." It helped to visualize the concept that educational success does not just occur at school or that the school's efforts were restricted to the time the students spent inside the building. The faculty truly wanted them to be successful all the time and wanted their families and parents to be successful with them.

In school it is essential that everything be connected to everything else. No endeavor or program should exist in isolation or separate from the rest of the school. This also is the philosophy behind the interdisciplinary teams in the middle schools. The teaching team monitors all activities of the team and sees to it that every experience supports the total educational effort. Students must see a connection between all of those educational efforts to which they are exposed. Our programs at Hazelwood Junior High School could have stood alone, isolated programs as they are in so many schools. However, they would not have been as effective.

Ensuring success for all students – a worthy goal for any middle level school and one that with conscientious effort is achievable. ▪S▪

# REFERENCES

Anderson, L.W., Cook, N.R., Pellicer, L.O., & Spradling, R.L. (1989). *A study of EIA-funded remedial and compensatory programs in South Carolina.* Columbia, SC: The South Carolina Educational Policy Center.

Arhar, J.M. (1992, Spring). Enhancing students' feelings of school membership: What principals can do. *Schools in the Middle,* 12-16.

Beane, J. A., & Lipka, R. P. (1986). *Self-concept, self-esteem, and the curriculum.* New York: Teachers College Press.

Beck, L., & Muria, J. (1980). A portrait of a tragedy: Research findings on the dropout. *High School Journal, 64,* 65-72.

Benning, D. (1992, May). Consideration in support of integrated education. Chicago, IL: Midwest Regional Center for Drug Free Schools and Communication and Chicago Area Office.

Bobbitt, W.L. (1977). When schools change. *Educational Leadership, 34* (6), 439-443.

Brodbelt, S. (1991, July/August). How tracking restricts educational opportunity. *The Clearing House,* 385-388.

Brubaker, D. (1991). A backstage view of at-risk students. *NASSP Bulletin, 75* (538), 59-66.

Bureau of the Census (1990). *Census of population and housing.* Washington, DC: The Bureau.

Calabrese, R.L. (1988, March). The structure of schooling and minority dropout rates. *The Clearing House.*

Callahan, R.C., & Long, V.O. (1983). Socialization and alienation: Perspectives on schooling. *The Clearing House, 56,* 418-420.

Campbell, L.P., & Flake, A.E. (1984, May). Latchkey children – what is the answer? *The Clearing House,* 381.

Carnegie Council on Adolescent Development (1989). *Turning points, Preparing American youth for the 21st century.* New York: Carnegie Corporation of New York.

Chavkin, N.F., & Williams, D.L. Jr. (1989). Low-income parents' attitudes toward parent involvement in education. *Journal of Sociology and Social Welfare, 47* (2).

Cole, R.W., Jr. (1983). Every home a school. *Phi Delta Kappan, 64* (6).

Cole, R.W., Jr. (1985). Sentinels for a modern age. *Phi Delta Kappan, 66* (8).

Comer, J.P. (1988, August). Connecting families and schools. *Drawing in the Family.* Denver: CO: Education Commission of the States.

Cooley, V.E. (1993). Tips for implementing a student assistance program. *NASSP Bulletin 76* (549), 10-20

Council on Middle Level Education (1985). *An agenda for excellence at the middle level.* Reston, VA: National Association of Secondary School Principals.

DeBlois, R. (1989). Keep at-risk students in school: Toward a curriculum for potential dropouts. *NASSP Bulletin, 73* (516), 6-12.

Dewey, J. (1933). *How we think.* Lexington, MA: D.C. Heath.

DuFour, R.P., & Schwartz, W. (1990). Addressing the tracking controversy by promoting educational opportunity. *NASSP Bulletin, 74* (530), 88-94.

Elam, S., Rose, L., & Gallup, A. (1996). The 28th annual Phi Delta Kappa/Gallup Poll of the public's attitude toward public schools. *Phi Delta Kappan, 78* (1), 41-59.

Epstein, J.L., & Connors, L.J. (1992, June). School and family partnerships. *NASSP Practitioner, 2-3.*

Fantini, M.D. (1986). *Regaining excellence in education.* Columbus, OH: Merrill.

Friedman, S.C. (1986, September 11). Death in park: Difficult questions for parents. *The New York Times,* p. A-1.

Gandara, P. (1989, January). Those children are ours: Moving toward a community. *NEA Today: Issues '89,* 38-43.

Garvin, J. P. (1988). What parents expect from middle schools. *Principal, 67* (4), 55-56.

Gastright, J. F. (1989). Don't base your dropout program on somebody else's problem. *Research Problem No. 8.* Phi Delta Kappa Center on Evaluation, Development, and Research,

Goodlad, J. (1984). *A place called school.* New York: McGraw Hill.

Hafner, A., Ingels, S., Schneider, B., & Stevenson, D. (1990). *A profile of the American eighth grader: NELS:88 student descriptive summary.* Washington, DC: National Center for Education Statistics, U.S. Department of Education.

Haskins, R., Walden, T., & Ramsey, C. (1983). Teachers and student behavior in high- and low-ability groups. *Journal of Educational Psychology, 75,* 865-876.

Henderson, A.T. (1988). *The evidence continues to grow: Parent involvement improves student achievement.* Columbia, MD: The National Committee for Citizens in Education.

Henderson, A.T., Marburger, C. L., & Ooms, T. (1986). *Beyond the bake sale: An educator's guide to working with parents.* Columbia, MD: The National Committee for Citizens in Education.

Hodgkinson, H.(1986). What's ahead for education? *Principal, 65*(3), 6-11.

Hood, M. (1992, Spring). Mentoring program provides nurturing atmosphere for all adolescents. *Schools in the Middle,* 20-22.

Hopfenberg, W. (1993). *The accelerated schools.* San Francisco: Jossey-Bass.

Jackard, C.R. (1988, November). Reaching the under-challenged, marginal, or at-risk student. *The Clearing House,* 128-130.

Kohn, A. (1991). Caring kids: The role of the school. *Phi Delta Kappan. 72*(7), 497-506.

Kuykendall, C. (1992). *From rage to hope: Strategies for reclaiming Black and Hispanic students.* Bloomington, IN: National Educational Service.

Levin, H. (1990, May 27). Quoted in, Teachers invited to stress positive, by Virginia Hick. *St. Louis Post Dispatch*, p. 8.

Mackey, J. (1977). Strategies for reducing adolescent alienation. *Educational Leadership. 34*(6), 449-452.

Mackey, J. (1978, May). Youth alienation in post-modern society. *High School Journal, 61,* 353-67.

Manning, M. Lee. (1985). What we need are effective students. *The Clearing House, May,* 380.

Maynard, W. (1977). Working with disruptive youth. *Educational Leadership, 34*(6), 417-421.

McLaughlin, M.W. (1988, August). Improving the home environment. *Drawing in the family. Family involvement in the schools.* Report No. ECS-PI-88-2. Denver, CO: Education Commission of the States.

National Institute of Education (1988). *Drawing in the family. Family involvement in the schools.* Report No. ECS-PI-88-2. Denver, CO: Education Commission of the States.

National Middle School Association (1995). *This we believe: Developmentally responsive middle level schools.* Columbus, OH: Author.

National Middle School Association (1995). *What is a middle school?* [Brochure]. Columbus, OH: Author.

Newman, F.M. (1989). Student engagement and high school reform. *Educational Leadership, 46* (5), 34-36.

Nieto, S. (1992). *Affirming diversity: The sociopolitical context of multicultural education.* New York: Longman.

Noland, T.K., & Taylor, B.L. (1986). *The effects of ability grouping: A meta-analysis of research findings.* (Eric Document Reproduction Service No. ED 269 451)

Oakes, J. (1985). *How schools structure inequality.* New Haven, CT: Yale University Press.

Office of Educational Research and Improvement (1987). *The current operation of the Chapter I program.* Washington DC: Author.

O'Neil, J. (1991). Working harder on schoolwork. *Education Update, 33* (1), 6-8.

Pigford, A. (1992, January/February). Solving the at-risk problem: Healthy schools can make the difference. *The Clearing House,* 156-158.

Pogrow, S. (1990). Challenging at-risk students: Findings from the HOTS Program. *Phi Delta Kappan, 71,* 389-397.

Poston, W. Jr., Stone, M., & Muther, C. (1992). *Making schools work.* Newbury Park, CA: Corwin Press, Inc.

Quest International (1988). *Skills for adolescence.* Granville, OH. Author.

Retzer, R. (1992). *Circle of friends: Key to promising future.* Excerpts from a speech given at the "Circle of Friends" Student Advisory Council retreat. Printed in *Newsletter, Midwest Regional Center for Drug-Free Schools and Communities and Chicago Area Office. May,* 5.

Rogus, J.F., & Wildenhaus, C. (1991). Programming for at-risk learners: A preventive approach. *NASSP Bulletin, 75,* (538), 1- 7.

Rowan, B., Guthrie, L., Lee, G., & Guthrie, G. (1986). *The design and implementation of Chapter I instructional services: A study of 24 schools.* San Francisco: Far West Laboratory of Educational Research and Development.

Schorr, L.B., with Daniel Schorr (1988). *Within our reach: Breaking the cycle of disadvantage.* New York: Doubleday.

Sinclair, R.L., & Ghory, W.J. (1987). *Reaching marginal students: A primary concern for school renewal.* Chicago: McCutchan Publishing Corporation.

Slavin, R.E. (1979). Integrating the desegregated classroom: Actions speak louder than words. *Educational Leadership. 36* (5), 322-326.

Slavin, R.E. (1989). Students at risk for school failure: The problem and its dimensions. In R.E. Slavin, N.L. Karweit, & N.A. Madden (Eds.), *Effective programs for students at risk.* Needham Heights, MA: Allyn and Bacon.

Sleeter, C.E., & Grant, C.A. (1986). Success for all students. *Phi Delta Kappan, 68* (4), 297-299.

Stevenson, C. (1992) *Teaching ten to fourteen year olds.* New York: Longman Publishing Group.

Strother, D. (1986). Dropping out. *Phi Delta Kappan 67,* 325-28.

Valencia, A. (1992). The minority at-risk student: An educational challenge. *The Journal of Educational Issues of Language Minority Students, 11.*

Wehlage, G.; Rutter, R.; Smith, G.; Lesko, N.; and Fernandez, R. (1989) *Reducing the risk: Schools as communities of support.* Philadelphia: Falmer Press.

Wheeler, H. (1991, March) *Reducing the perceptions of racism through a student leadership forum.* Speech given at NASSP National Convention. Orlando, FL.

## NATIONAL MIDDLE SCHOOL ASSOCIATION

National Middle School Association was established in 1973 to serve as a voice for professionals and others interested in the education of young adolescents. The Association has grown rapidly and now enrolls members in all fifty states, the Canadian provinces, and forty-two other nations. In addition, fifty-three state, regional, and provincial middle school associations are official affiliates of NMSA.

NMSA is the only association dedicated exclusively to the education, development, and growth of young adolescents. Membership is open to all. While middle level teachers and administrators make up the bulk of the membership, central office personnel, college and university faculty, state department officials, other professionals, parents, and lay citizens are also actively involved in supporting our single mission – improving the educational experiences of 10-15 year olds. This open and diverse membership is a particular strength of NMSA.

The Association provides a variety of services, conferences, and materials in fulfilling its mission. In addition to *Middle School Journal*, the movement's premier professional journal, the Association publishes *Research in Middle Level Education Quarterly*, a wealth of books and monographs, videos, an association newsletter, a magazine, and occasional papers. The Association's highly acclaimed annual conference, which has drawn over 10,000 registrants in recent years, is held in the fall.

For information about NMSA and its many services contact the Headquarters at 2600 Corporate Exchange Drive, Suite 370, Columbus, Ohio 43231, TELEPHONE 800-528-NMSA, FAX 614-895-4750.